The Great Game
of Networking

The Great Game
of Networking

✦

Simple, fun, actionable strategies for
becoming a networking all-star!

Dr. Burt Smith, CME, CQM, PCM

iUniverse, Inc.
New York Lincoln Shanghai

The Great Game of Networking
Simple, fun, actionable strategies for becoming a networking all-star!

iUniverse books may be ordered through booksellers or by contacting:

iUniverse
2021 Pine Lake Road, Suite 100
Lincoln, NE 68512
www.iuniverse.com
1-800-Authors (1-800-288-4677)

Because of the dynamic nature of the Internet, any Web addresses or links contained in this book may have changed since publication and may no longer be valid.

The information, ideas, and suggestions in this book are not intended to render professional advice. Before following any suggestions contained in this book, you should consult your personal accountant or other financial advisor. Neither the author nor the publisher shall be liable or responsible for any loss or damage allegedly arising as a consequence of your use or application of any information or suggestions in this book.

ISBN: 978-0-595-45772-4 (pbk)
ISBN: 978-0-595-90074-9 (ebk)

Printed in the United States of America

For my wife, Terri, who I met thanks to networking! Just when I thought our life couldn't get any better, she gave me a son that I can't stop talking about.

... for Dalton, who was born while I was writing this, or it would have been on the shelves 6 months earlier! This is the first of many things I hope he'll be proud of!

... to his grandfather, Tom, that he never got to meet, and to his Grandma Wanda who has vowed to spoil him rotten!

... and to God above for the grace he showed by letting me be raised in Roger Mills County, Oklahoma, where the population is small but the encouragement is monumental.

Contents

Introduction

Welcome to Your Future!

There are three key factors that will determine your success in life: What you know, who knows you, and your ability to take action!

I share that philosophy in front of just about every audience I've addressed, whether it's a group of sales professionals who are looking for ways to reach more prospects, a group of graduating high school seniors and their parents, small business owners who are seeking maximization of their personal sales and marketing efforts, or even a group of employees whose future may be uncertain because of a pending corporate restructure. The philosophy is time-honored, relevant, and frighteningly true. What we know (our training/education) is a critical success factor, giving us the competence and the credibility to accomplish our goals. Who we know, and more importantly, making sure they know us, helps us get our foot in the door so we can put that training and education to work and reap our own benefits while helping others. And to accomplish anything we have to be willing to take action. Just having the skills isn't good enough. We have to be willing to apply what we learn by taking action.

This book is about educating you in the how-to's of networking, helping you use those skills to make sure people who can help you know who you are, and about ensuring you have the skills and encouragement you need to take the actions necessary to make it happen.

Welcome to the great game of networking! I say that because once you hone and perfect the skills of professional networking, you'll find that "work" becomes a lot less like work and a whole lot more fun because you're making friends, helping people and making a good living as a result of doing so.

I learned these things firsthand from my own experiences. I discovered the power of networking long before I even knew what "networking" was. You see, in a little town like where I'm from, when someone needs a product or service, they don't necessarily go to the phone book and try to find a solution. They start asking around. "Hey, who do you know who does roofing?" a resident might ask a neighbor they run into at the grocery store or post office. The recommendation will typically be derived from the respondent's, or someone else's, experience. "I don't know right offhand, but I know so-and-so had a new roof put on last year and they used such-and-such company. I'll ask them what they thought and find out how they liked them."

I was amazed, once my career and yearning for adventure took me out of my hometown of Roll, Oklahoma (population 36) and into the world of business, how the power of personal connections and word-of-mouth recommendations still trumped even the most sophisticated promotional strategies in their effectiveness. Most of the time, even with the vast amounts of information so readily available to us, and in direct avoidance of the nearly 3,000 advertising messages to which Americans are exposed daily, we still depend on human interaction to help us make our purchase decisions. Companies spend billions of dollars on advertising to spread messages and tell their stories, but human beings still look to other human beings they know, and whose opinions they respect, to help guide them through the decision-making process. This is one role played by networking, and it is powerful stuff.

Another reason I so passionately endorse the great game of networking is because it is incredibly fun to meet your goals, thanks to the help of others, and to have the satisfaction of knowing you helped your fellow network members, too. As hard as our careers can be and as much of our daily lives as we have to spend involved in our "work," I think it should be as much fun as possible. If you think about those you admire and probably those you want most to be around, they are probably people who are very passionate about what they do and seem to have a lot of fun doing it. This is a great lesson for us. Get good at the great game of networking and you'll never "work" again!

> *"Many people think amateurs do not play for money, but play for the love of the game. In reality, the reason amateurs are amateurs is because they do not love the game enough."*—Steven Pressfield, *The War of Art*

One Goal, One Skill, One Contact!

Before we get down to business, let's talk about what's in it for you, and how to get the most from this or any book that offers to train you in a new skill or help you enhance your current repertoire. First, realize that you should set one specific goal any time you read a book, attend a lecture or seminar, or basically engage in any activity. That goal is ONE THING. Set for yourself the goal of getting at least *one thing* from this book that will help you and I'll bet you'll see a significant return on your investment. Try it!

Along those same lines, you may in reality be only one skill away from meeting the one contact that helps all your goals become profitable realities! Once you start playing the great game of networking, you'll see how remarkably true that is! You may have to develop a lot of skills before that one magic skill makes it happen, and you may have to meet a lot of people before you meet that one power-connection that creates a point of inflection for your career and rockets you on your way, but it really could come down to that. In fact, to really put yourself in the right frame of mind, every networking luncheon you attend could be considered your "Million Dollar Lunch." There might be ONE person there whose acquaintance could result in you eventually getting everything you ever wanted. And the more skills you have to help you meet that person, the greater the likelihood of it happening.

Never will I promise this is the best or only book on networking you should read. Far from it! A professional like you should get as vast an exposure to as many resources that can help you as you can. I will promise that anyone, from any experience level, can get at least ONE very powerful idea from this book that will pay off. I'll not only promise that, I'll guarantee it or refund the purchase price of this book. Details on that are included in the back of the book. And even if you think this is the greatest book on networking you ever read, I will still recommend some to you, so you can maximize your potential. I'm still reading and growing, and I hope long after we part ways here you and I can both say the same. I also hope you'll find my booklist on my website a helpful, ongoing resource. And I hope if there are titles that should be added that you don't see there, you'll share them so you and I and OUR fellow networking professionals can benefit.

1

What Is "Networking?"

What is Networking?

It's far less important what you know, than who knows you! I said earlier that who you know is potentially more important than what you know, and to take that a step further, it's really more essential that we understand how important it is, that not only that you know people, but that *they* know *you*. And it's critical that when they think about whatever it is you "do" (products you sell, job you're seeking, purpose/cause you represent, mission you're on, etc.), that they think first of you, instead of another solution to their problem or cause in which they could invest their time, money, and/or energy. So it's not so much who you know, but *who knows you*!

That's where "networking" comes in. We're talking about a network of human resources. People who are in a position to help you reach your goals and are willing to do so, because they know you'd do the same for them.

To take it even further, I believe networking is a means of personal branding. You are the brand, you are the product, you are the message, and your networking activity gives you the opportunity to customize, share, and spread your branding message in very effective ways. That's the strategy we'll use in this book. If you are the manager of a sales force or the owner of an organization, or are otherwise responsible for sending team members into the world to represent your organization, I hope you'll give some very serious thought to this philosophy and share it with your employees, family members, and anyone else who potentially represents your brand in any situation. Remind them that, to the people they meet, they *are* the organization. They are the window through which the organization is viewed. They are the brand, they are YOUR brand, and you should make sure they're trained accordingly.

Once reserved only for the affluent

Successful people have always understood the value of having a strong network; However, in the not too distant past, the great game of networking was accessible only by the affluent who had country club connections and a big Rolodex (you may be too young to remember what Rolodex's were … think of it as an antique Blackberry!) of people they could call on for favors, or to whom they could calculatingly share favors. The rest of us didn't mind so much, because in the old days we all pretty much found a job or career we were happy with and expected to stay there for 20 or 30 years until we retired. Starting in about 1990, though, we discovered that the notion of working for one firm or even solely in one industry for the entire lifespan of a career was a plan subject to change, and not by our choice. Companies began to inject frightening words into our vocabularies: Downsize, rightsize, reengineer, realignment, and so on. It often meant that many lost their jobs and the "lucky ones" were left overworked in positions that didn't really thrill them, and they had difficulty knowing where, or to whom, to turn for a better set of circumstances. Placement firms were flooded with the resumes of the displaced, and the law of supply and demand pushed many of those resumes to the bottom of the stack. Those who had "contacts," however, often fared much better.

Before we even get started, I suggest that regardless of how happy or secure you feel where you are today, even if you own the business, you are well advised to build a network so, if you end up in a position like that, though I sincerely hope you never do, you'll have a potential margin of safety. A network can give you choices, and choices can give you peace of mind.

I don't mean to make it sound like the 1990s were some decade of doom. Many of those who were displaced actually improved their circumstances by being motivated (I've fortunately never been canned, but I'm sure it's strong motivation!) to find an even better job they perhaps wouldn't have sought otherwise. The number of small businesses started in the 1990s soared thanks, in many cases, to such life-changing events. The difference between success and failure is rarely dependent just on the situation, but on how the person affected deals with the situation. The more tools the individual has, the better able he or she is to make the situation work for them.

The great game of networking changed significantly in the 1990s. This extraordinary tool was made available to those who had the gumption to take advantage of the opportunity! Today, networking remains a powerful asset for those who like to control their own destinies. A poll by Robert Half & Associates showed 48% of professionals are doing more networking today than in years past. Every indication is that, regardless of the role technology will ultimately play in business and even in networking itself, the fundamental ability to network will remain a crucial skill among professionals.

Not-for-Profits and Students Need Apply!

The tone and language of this book is probably a little biased toward "business" readers. You'll hear me use terms like "prospect," "customer," "lead," "referral," etc. However, the principles taught in this book can potentially benefit ANYONE who needs the cooperation of others. A student who is about to enter the workforce for the first time may be able to leapfrog right over other candidates just by making the right contact who can help them get the job they seek. In fact, merely playing the great game of networking may help the student who wants to become employed because so few students take such initiative.

Similarly, the members of a not-for-profit, governmental agency, or any other cause will also benefit from networking skills. Until very recently, the idea that a not-for-profit organization had a "product" to "sell" or that they were a "brand" of any kind was a foreign concept. That has changed dramatically over the past few years, and continues to change, especially as competition for support has increased. Advancing your cause is important to you, and you'll find that the techniques you learn in this book can help you increase awareness for your organization and, much more importantly, help you secure valuable contributions in the form of donations and volunteer support (action!). And of course, all of those things are just means to helping you accomplish the real goal, which is to help the people your cause serves. Networking is all about creating win-win relationships in which value is exchanged for both parties. We know your cause has value, so look forward to letting the great game of networking cost-effectively help you share that message with the world and get as many individuals and organizations involved as possible. Networking is far too powerful a tool not to put to work for your mission and your stakeholders!

How Big a Network Are We Talking About?

We each know about 250 people, on average. Some know a lot more, some know fewer. If you were pressed to write down the names of all the people with whom you are acquainted you could probably list over 200 very easily, or you may go well above 300. If you doubt this, check out your Christmas card list or the list of guests you invited to your wedding or other important event. When we network, we have the opportunity not only to make those 250 people we know stewards of our brand and champions for us, but to tap into the 250 or so people each of them knows. As you can see, your efforts have the potential to grow exponentially.

In fact, you should never be more than about four contacts away from solving any problem you or another member of your network have. You can become the problem solver in your community and enjoy incredible personal brand equity as a result. One time, several years ago, after I had just begun to seriously play the great game of networking, I got a call from one of my clients who happened to be in the insurance business. He was looking for awnings for his office. Remember, he is my client, so how he was associating my market research and consulting practice with awnings had me starting to worry a little about my own marketing! How in the world did he make that connection? He went on to explain that yes, he fully understood that I wasn't in the awning business, but he knew my business was marketing and he also knew I knew a lot of people. I did an aggie high five (that's where you forcefully smack yourself in the forehead) and said to myself, "No kidding! I am not just his marketing consultant, I'm his problem solver! I want to be known as the guy who's "connected," which is exactly why you're reading this book right now! I then remembered that just the previous day I had been at a luncheon with a vendor who does signs for business. I told my client I'd do some checking and get back to him later that day. I called the vendor I knew who did signs, and he told me they didn't do awnings, but he did know someone whom he would confidently recommend. I then got the information and called my client within the hour. He was obviously very appreciative. I had not only solved his problem, I'd helped him save time, which is exactly the kind of service I want my clients to associate with me. Four phone calls, problem solved, client satisfied, expeditiously done deal, everybody wins.

The story gets better, though! When I ran into my client at the next luncheon of a group we both belonged to, he greeted me with a huge smile and made a point of introducing me to the group of five other professionals he was talking to and told them the story, making your old buddy Dr. Burt sound like the best thing since the hula hoop! "This guy knows how to get things done!" My client told them. "He can solve your problem!" This intrigued the group enough to engage me in not only a discussion of how I do indeed help solve the problems of businesses and help them increase profits, but one of the five became a client for my customer satisfaction research service!

That was over 12 years ago. I have lots of similar stories, but that one is my favorite because it was the first personal demonstration I'd had in the awesome power of networking. These are the kinds of win-win relationships that await you as you play the great game of networking! I can't wait for you to experience them! In the words of my Canadian friends, "Exciting, eh?"

2

Where Can You Play The Great Game of Networking?

Where Can Networking Take Place?

The short answer is ANYWHERE! Anywhere can be a networking opportunity. There are several groups whose specific purpose is to provide networking and professional development opportunities. Some examples are discussed below.

Chambers of Commerce

Chambers of Commerce can be excellent sources of networking. Most have events of one kind or another going on year-round, and often provide networking-specific activities for the benefit of their members because they recognize the power of putting their members in touch with one another. I often hear a lot of criticism of the typical chamber of commerce-sponsored networking event. Investigation usually reveals that this is because the attendees just expect the networking to "happen" and it doesn't. In fact, the media used for the promotion of the event usually states something like "There will be lots of networking." That is not quite true. The professional networker, YOU, has to take the initiative. Perhaps a more accurate way most organizations could promote networking events would be to advertise that networking opportunities will be *available* or *possible,* rather than to say "there will be plenty of networking," and imply that you'll be met with some great group hug and people holding out bags for you to drop your business card into like kids trick-or-treating. Networking is not supplied by anyone, it is created. As we'll discuss in the following pages, a networking opportunity can be created by a professional like YOU just about anywhere.

Professional/Trade Associations

Similar to the Chamber of Commerce, there are tons of professional and trade associations that both serve the profession and those who are stakeholders in the profession. For example, the American Marketing Association, my all-time favorite professional organization (<u>www.</u>

marketingpower.com), has the mission of serving those whose profession is marketing, such as advertising agencies, graphic designers, and educators. But their membership is also open to the printers who sell to the advertising agencies, suppliers of computers, direct mail suppliers, and a host of other vendors who support the marketers. Doing a search in your area of "associations" may reveal some great venues for networking, and you'll probably find most have a type of "associate" membership available to you, even if you are not considered a member of the profession or trade.

Obviously if you choose a group or association that represents your profession, you will find some of your competitors there. You will also find that if you really get to know most of your competitors, you'll find that though you are indeed members of the same profession, you may not be "competitors." If you find out exactly who is a prospect for one another, you may find that by forming strategic alliances you can create win-win relationships and you can both maximize your promotional efforts. Even the biggest of companies can't do all the business, and having dependable strategic partners to whom they can partner or refer business can be a great way to grow the brands of both organizations.

If they turn out to be jerks, consider it a compliment because that means they're really threatened by you and that you're doing something right! Keep doing what you're doing and remember that you don't want jerks in your network, anyway!

Civic Groups

There are a lot of groups that exist to serve a civic purpose: Lions Club, Rotary, Kiwanis, Junior League, are just a few that come to mind. To help accomplish their mission, their membership consists of go-getters like you who can get things done. What great places these are to network, because the membership consists of community leaders and those who aspire to be community leaders. You may find a lot of professional and personal rewards for your involvement with your choice of a Civic Group.

Some groups with international ties, like Rotary, give you the opportunity to network all over the world. What I enjoyed most about Rotary was the ability to visit other, larger clubs in my area and be treated so nicely as a guest.

In fact, if you have your eye on Rotary, here's a little tip to help you maximize your investment: Join a small club! You get all the benefits of being plugged into a worldwide organization, and you'll have more leadership opportunities within the smaller club. But the best thing about joining a smaller Rotary club is that you get to visit the larger clubs, where dues are more expensive, as a guest. In fact, as a guest, they will introduce you and you get to stand and be recognized! I always thought it was kind of funny when I'd visit these larger clubs where one tends to get lost in the shuffle if he or she is a member, but as a guest you get introduced every time you attend! That is some great exposure and by paying smaller dues at a smaller chapter, you're able to stretch the value of your investment.

Tips Clubs

Though these are my least favorite venue because they don't seem to sustain themselves, tips clubs can be a great source of networking. You're surrounded with people who are looking to accomplish their goals, but the structure of the group usually requires that they give as much as they receive in terms of referrals and "tips." Unfortunately, we all have a limited number of referrals we can or feel comfortable giving, so the well seems to run dry on the typical tips club fairly soon in most cases. However, you be the judge. Consider test driving some of the tips clubs in your area to see what kind of feel you get for them.

Legislative Events

Most legislators need to get out and press flesh at least a few times during their terms. In some areas your state or local Chamber of Commerce may actually sponsor such an event. If so, you will definitely want to attend one of these. Leaders, the kind of people you want in your network, often take an active, prominent role in the political process. Though "networking" isn't the specific agenda, you will find yourself in the presence of those who may be of help to you and would make valuable members of your network. At the very least, you want to make sure your legislators are members of your network because serving you is their job. You never know when you might need them. Attending legislative events shows you are a professional who takes an active role in the political process and that can bolster your brand. I recommend attending as many of these as your time and pocketbook allow, and be seen frequently by your political leaders so they will know you well if you ever show up in their office with a need. Their recognizing you *first* at events helps your brand, too!

Something for the Professional to Consider

It's worth pointing out that just because the group or organization doesn't claim to be a "networking" group does not mean there are no networking opportunities. Remember, networking opportunities are *created* by professional networkers like you, not granted by some organization. As we said earlier, whether any actual networking takes place is up to professionals like you who actually take action and get out there and do it. Here are some other places where you can make networking happen:

Seminars & workshops

Professionals like you are always looking for ways to better themselves, and you probably find yourself at quite a few seminars. Can you think of a better crowd with whom to network? These are movers and shakers like you! They are taking their time and probably even their own money to attend a workshop or seminar, so they see the value of continuous improvement. Chances are they are respected in their fields, just like you, so they are the kinds of folks you want added to your network. These are the caliber of individuals you want championing for you and for whom you can do the same. So, don't go just for the program, take your own networking agenda to any seminar or workshop you attend. Always be networking!

Social Gatherings

The reason we attend a social gathering is to "socialize," and that is something we should always bear in mind. On the other hand, people like to help people they like, so the better your ability to take a genuine interest in other people in a social situation, the more likely they are to want to know what you do and the more eager they will be to help you accomplish your goals.

For all you know, the person you're sitting next to at your child's soccer game could either help you reach your goals, or knows someone you need to know. Be professional, be friendly, and be prepared at all times to play, with passion, the great game of networking. You'll find the guiding principles we discuss on exactly how to handle any networking situation can also be modified to fit any social situation in which you find yourself.

But ...

Just because anywhere CAN be a networking opportunity, does that mean it should be? Nope. Obviously there are some places which appear to be excellent networking opportunities, but our professional integrity will keep them from being networking opportunities.

The funeral of the most prominent person in town will draw a crowd of excellent prospects, but ...

You could drop your business card in the offering plate at church or give your priest a sales pitch in the confessional, but ...

One final thing ...

Because anywhere *can* be a networking opportunity, not only should you be the best professional networker you can be, it's not a bad idea to give your spouse, children, friends, and anyone else who could potentially be a promoter for you a little lesson in what you do and what others should know about what you do. This is really not that hard to do and can pay off incredibly. They can become what Guy Kawasaki, author of *How to Drive Your Competition Crazy* calls "customer evangelists." Many of the techniques you'll read about in this book can and should be taught to those folks who can help build your brand within their personal networks. Make sure they know what you do so they can help you deliver your valuable message to the people they know.

3

*Preparing to Play the Great
Game of Networking*

Gearing up

So we've recognized the potential rewards awaiting us from our networking activities. We'll now focus on both the strategic and tactical moves needed to effectively play the game—The *great* game of networking!

3 keys:

1. **ALWAYS carry your business cards with you**
2. **Develop a marketing statement**
3. **Choose your arenas**

Business Cards

It goes without saying that you have to have business cards to play the great game of networking, but there are a couple of things that are worth mentioning. First, always … and I do mean *always*, have your business cards with you. Second, make sure you make the most of the promotional power of your business cards.

Always. Always, always, always carry your business cards with you. In case that didn't come across strongly enough, let me state again—ALWAYS carry your business cards! You never know when a networking opportunity may present itself, so you need to be ready at all times. Your business cards are tools of the trade, so make sure you're always ready to participate in, or even *create*, your own networking opportunities by having the necessary equipment to play the game.

I heard of a fellow one time who had a running bet that if he was ever caught without his business cards, he would pay the person who caught him $50. As you can imagine, this earned him a sort of celebrity status. He always had people catching him at the grocery store, the post office, when he was gassing up his car, and so on, checking to see if he had his business cards. I heard once he even had someone approach him in the sauna at the health club and thought they had him. He simply produced a sealed plastic bag and handed the person a business card! I never found out from exactly *where* he produced the plastic sealed bag but that's another story, and I may not want to know! According to legend, never in the entire time he did this did he ever have to pay anyone the $50. Obviously when he showed up at an "official" networking event, people recognized him and he often attracted a small mob until it was discovered he had his business card on his person. It also begged the questions from the observers who hadn't yet met the gentleman, "What's all that about? What does that guy do? Who is that?" and other questions that earned the fellow enough attention to potentially engage those in attendance in a discussion of exactly what he does and why it was of benefit to the attendees. This is what we'll discuss in upcoming sections. You'll see how you can create that kind of buzz for yourself just by helping others. In the mean time, please complete this sentence so I'll know our time in this section has been a good investment in your networking career:

Always carry your _____.

Bravo! Now here are a few tips on how to make the most effective use of your business cards.

Because your business cards are literally the tools of the networking trade, it's imperative to make the most effective use of them. You're probably more than capable of designing your own business cards, but I'd strongly encourage you to make sure you have a professional help you. This could be as formal as an ad agency who designs cards, letterhead, thank-you notes, and a set of collateral materials which give you a consistent look, or as informal as going to a print shop, but I do encourage you to get another set of well trained, well experienced eyes to help you in creating your business cards. After all, this is an investment in your overall brand.

You can, and should, get creative with your cards. A great example of getting creative with your cards is provided by one of my favorite marketing gurus, Terri Langhans. You can see this and even purchase one for yourself at www.blahblahblah.us . What she does is turn her cards into a miniature version of her presentation. Not only are these great promotional pieces, but she says people rarely throw them away because they are so neat. She'll get calls from people years after she's met them just because they've kept her business card so close to them. When they need a speaker or consultant, Terri is often top-of-mind with them, because they remember how clever and helpful her promotional piece was.

Another friend of mine who has a direct mail business literally makes his card into a mini-brochure. The card looks like a regular business card on front, which includes his logo, contact info, all the things you'd see on the typical business card, but that's where it stops being typical and starts being a component of his brand. Because they like to showcase themselves as not just a typical "mail house," but instead as a key part of their clients' marketing strategies, the card is constructed like an envelope. The envelope opens and folds out into a mini-brochure that *demonstrates*, not just describes, the reasons why his firm should be his clients' vendor of choice.

My friend and fellow speaker, John Storm, speaks on creativity. His business card not only gives you some great reasons to hire him and multiple ways to get in touch with him, but also some valuable takeaways. It folds out not into a brochure, but into a summary of some of his tips on being creative. In fact, it's a sort of mini-workshop (or at least a refresher) right there in his card. Like Terri Langhans' card, it's impossible to throw away! Even though I see John regularly and have all his info in my database (something you'll want to do with your contacts too, and we'll discuss in a later section), I am compelled to keep his valuable card and refer to it any time I need a creativity recharge. You can visit www.thebookonbrainstorming.com and John will probably send you one so you can see for yourself.

If you've ever heard Jeffrey Gitomer speak, or read one of his books, you know he is anything but traditional! So it's not surprising that rather than carry a traditional business card, he carries what he calls a "coin card." It's a small coin with all his relevant information on it. Prospects who receive this are impressed with its uniqueness. They not only have something that anchors who Jeff is and what he does with something unique, but tend to hang on to his card and show others. I've not yet had the chance to meet Jeff and ask him, but I'll bet it'd do him proud if you took that idea and ran with it.

Check out www.burtmarketing.com now and then to see if there are other tips and resources to help you in this regard. If you have a hall-of-fame idea you want to share, I'd love to hear it and feature you in a later book.

At the very least, I encourage you to stop thinking of your card as just a piece of paper and, instead, think of it as a crucial component of your brand. Design your card as a mini-brochure. You can do this very simply by making good use of the back of your business card. Jay Conrad Levinson, author of the popular Guerilla Marketing series, shared this advice way back in the 1980s and I've used it since then, but I'm still surprised at how few organizations take advantage of this very cost-effective promotional idea. Some things you could put on the back of your card include, but may not be limited to:

- Bullet points outlining product offerings
- Short statements of benefit
- Your web address
- Your corporate mission
- Something of benefit to the recipient (calendar, metric conversion table, government holidays, sports schedules, etc.)
- A mini-resume (if you're a student or someone seeking a job)

Some of the members of my network say they don't like using the back of their business cards because they use the backs of the cards they get from people, when networking, to write notes about the person they've met, and they don't want to use that space in case the people they give their cards want to use the space to make notes. I have a very important follow-up step that I'll discuss in a later section of the book that I believe addresses this and makes a case for using the back of your card for promotional reasons. I just think that the back of your business cards is valuable ad space that may be going to waste. Maybe something like this is a compromise for the back of your business cards:

Use this space to write notes about how we can help each other ...

That way you encourage those who receive your business cards to actively engage in taking notes about who you are, and what you do. I still think there are better uses for your business cards and I think you'll see that too when I revisit how we *use* our business cards in a later section.

In any case, a printer can help you. Better yet, if you're working with a graphic artist, promotional products firm, or advertising agency, they can help you develop cards, logos, letterhead, your website, etc. so your brand will be consistent. If you don't have those kinds of contacts yet, look forward to meeting them in your networking. Just make sure you get the maximum benefit from your business cards! And in case I haven't mentioned it yet, always make sure you have them with you!

The Marketing Statement

We need to think very seriously about what we'll say once we are "on-sight" and playing the great game of networking. This is where the marketing statement comes in. Some authors call this the Unique Selling Proposition (USP) or the Statement of Benefit, or something more clever than the "marketing statement," but they're all pretty much the same thing and since they deal with marketing, that's what I call it.

I've had varied success in my workshops taking time to have participants develop their marketing statements. Some participants have remarkable moments of clarity and a valuable marketing statement appears to them on the spot, they wow us all, and they are able to profitably use it from now on. I pat myself on the back in front of the audience and do my best to convince them all that my ingenious facilitation helped the miracle happen. On the other hand, many of us don't think and create most effectively in that kind of setting, so we come away from the experience without a marketing statement and feel like it's something beyond our grasp because we're not creative enough. As a result, what I've done instead in my workshops, and will do for you here, is to say that the best way to develop a magical marketing statement is to think long and hard about it, research it thoroughly, test it with as many people as you can, keep lots and lots of notes, capture every idea, then relax and wait for it to appear.

Marketing Journal Exercise

Starting NOW, keep a journal of any and all good marketing ideas you see. Jot it down along with a brief description of why you thought it was a good idea and any other relevant information about the idea you think you may need to help remember it. Most successful people I know keep both personal journals and "idea journals" and find they may use an idea they listed in their journals several years earlier! So don't just list the idea, give yourself a little explanation and rationale on why you included it. That way, when you review you'll recall why you wanted to keep it.

These ideas can help in all aspects of your marketing, but a journal housing them all is especially helpful in aiding you in your creation of a powerful marketing statement. If you see a good tagline or hear an action word you think would work for you, jot it down. You'll be surprised what this does for your creative processes.

In the meantime, here's a straightforward approach you can take to developing the first draft of your marketing statement.

A simple fill in the blanks approach

Start by answering the following questions:

1. We are _____ (the name of your company)

2. We help _____ (who you serve)

3. We do this by _____ (how)

In practice, I have actually tended to state my benefit first, then my name, then that of my company. This is the result of having attended many meetings where attendees are allowed to introduce themselves and having experienced what marketing has taught us for a number of years. People care more about benefits than features. My name and that of my company are features. The benefit is what I can do for anyone listening to my marketing statement. It is the value I can provide and it is why they should care. I prefer to state the benefit first, hoping that spurs interest so they are more attentive when I give my name and my company name, hoping they'll remember at least one if we have no further contact or they do a keyword search on the web or something later on. It goes like this:

We help organizations increase profits by helping them measure and improve customer satisfaction. We are Executive Marketing Information, and my name is Burt Smith.

I experiment with new things once and a while and will modify or even replace a statement altogether, but that one has consistently performed for me and I know you'll find one that delivers for you as well.

Here's another example. I've heard an accountancy who works with independently owned businesses use this statement:

We help companies make more money and keep more of what they make.

That one grabs attention and opens a dialogue. Short, simple, gets right to the point, and it immediately involves the listener, who may ask, "I know an accountant can help save me money in reduced taxes, but *make* me more money? How do you do that?" The accountant can then go on to explain that yes, they do help small businesses minimize their tax liability, but their firm is different because, as their accountant, they are intimately involved with the workings of the client's business. As such, they can help spot opportunities to save money and be more efficient. This helps improve the client's bottom line, and by helping them *keep more of what they make*, they are essentially making giving the client a raise. They can explain that the client *makes* more money by being more efficient. This is not the whole sales presentation, but it is an attention getter. It's just enough information to intrigue the potential client into wanting to know more, and creates the opportunity for a more official meeting at an appropriate time. Even if that meeting doesn't take place for some time or never takes place, the listener has just met an accountant they are likely to remember and can refer.

The key again is, don't beat yourself up or put yourself on the sidelines of the great game of networking just because you don't have the magic statement yet. Success is a process, not an event. It has to evolve.

Keep after it and you'll eventually have one that wows us all and puts more money in your pocket.

Here's some space for you to jot any notes that may have come to mind as you craft your marketing statement. A good place to start is to think not so much about what you "do," but how that *benefits* those for whom you do it and how you are *different* from or are a *better* choice than those in your field who provide the same product or service. Benefits are what people buy, so be sure your statement revolves around how you help!

NOTES

_____

_____

_____

_____

_____

_____

_____

_____

Choosing an Arena

Picking with great deliberation the arenas in which we are going to play the great game of networking is a critical decision. This is because regardless of the size of our organization or promotional resources, those resources ultimately have limits. Even though networking itself is largely "free," which is one reason I love it so, we are limited in the amount of time we have to commit to the great game of networking. In fact, if you haven't already realized that time is your most precious resource, I hope you'll let me share that lesson with you now. Time is infinitely more important than money or any other resource. We can always make more money, but we cannot manufacture more time.

Once it's gone, it's gone, and we need to be very stingy with how we use our time. Choosing where and when to conduct our networking is an important decision in that regard.

Having said that, how do we go about choosing the arenas in which we conduct our networking? Optimally, of course, we'll be spending our time networking with those individuals who are qualified prospects or decision makers in our target market. Investing our time in ways that put us closest to decision makers from our exact target market should be our top priority, so seeking out those kinds of venues is where we should start.

Exercise

Think about groups you're familiar with, and imagine who in that group can be of help to you. Better yet, think up some specific questions to ask representatives from groups you're considering:

1. How many members are in this organization?

2. How many events or activities do they have where members attend in groups?

3. About how many people usually attend these events (all members rarely attend, and most organizations allow non-members to attend a few events)?

4. How many events can I attend before I join?

5. What are the specific reasons I should join? (Make them earn your business!)

6. Other questions:_____

   _____

   _____

   _____

   _____

You're tapping into their networks

They say we each know about 250, or so, people. Chances are, a mover and shaker like you knows a lot more, and some shier people know less, but if we had to average the numbers out, it would shake out to around 250 on average. (My source on this is "They," by the way). Seriously, though, if we really were pressed to sit down and list all the people we know (relatives, coworkers, friends, friends of friends, etc.), we'd be very surprised at how many names we could list. Granted, these names might not be folks we know well enough to loan money or ask us to help move, but they are at least people we know.

This is an extremely important detail to note because we must always remember that regardless of where or with whom we're networking, regardless of their backgrounds or power as decision makers, we are tapping into their network of 250, or so, people. What that tells us is we need to be on our best networking behavior at all times. The person we're talking to at the moment may not be a prospect for our offer, but there is a strong possibility they know someone who is, and may even have significant influence with that person.

Hint: A good question to ask frequently of people with whom you network is, "What other organizations are you using?" You can find out what meetings they attend, whether they have joined or not, if they have joined, whether it is worth it or not, and of course, if they would recommend it. They might even be willing to take you as their guest at the next meeting (especially if you make a point of asking them!).

Don't join until they make you!

Something I strongly advocate is attending various groups as often as possible before writing the organization a check to become a member. This lets you "test drive" the organization before you make an investment that could commit your time and money for a year or so. It also lets you perhaps make enough valuable contacts to recoup the costs of joining. If an organization is a serious one, and they are seriously seeking your membership, they will allow you to attend a few times for free. If they are really committed to the success of their members, they'll help you meet enough people, or otherwise obtain value from the time you attend as a non-member, to such a degree that you will eagerly write them a check and join. There are always membership drives, contests, or what have you, offering rewards for members attracting other members, and larger organizations may actually monetarily compensate an executive director or sales force for getting members. I say, make them earn it! After all, you and I have to!

I had actually stopped using the "Don't join until they make you" story in my workshops because it sounded a little stingy. That was until a person who had attended one several years ago came up to me and told me her ability to effectively "shop" organizations before joining had saved her thousands of dollars over her career. Because you are the one paying for this book, I believe I have an obligation to advise you to attend as many meetings of any organization as possible before committing to any long-term investment. So don't join until you are confident in the return on your investment. *Don't join until they make you!*

Write down the names of some organizations to research and/or visit, as you consider arenas in which you'll play the great game of networking:

4

The Big 10 Guiding Principles of the Great Game of Networking

The "Big 10"

We've practiced our marketing statements, we've had our business cards redone to utilize the back side as a marketing tool, we've done some informal research with our friends or peers to see what sounds best to them, and we've chosen some arenas we want to try out. Now we're ready to do what separates the successful from the dreamers: Take *action*!

In the following section you'll become familiar with 10 "Guiding Principles" I've developed for any networking situation. I call these "Guiding Principles," rather than "Hard & Fast Rules," because they are just that: *Guiding* principles. They don't go in any kind of entirely linear format, you don't have to do one and not do the other, and you may find that what I'm suggesting doesn't work for you, but causes you to think of something that would. That's the idea. They are guiding principles designed to help you navigate the field as you play the great game of networking, so learn them well but use them as you see fit.

These are principles, however, I developed through nearly 20 years of networking on my own, from my own formal and informal study, and from my own experiences, so I'm also very confident that if you actively try to make each work for you, (and by work for you I mean take it, tailor it, and make it your own), you'll see great results for your networking efforts.

#1: You're There to Professionally Network, NOT to Hand Out Business Cards!

As you are engaged in the great game of networking, watch for these annoying people. They'll make their way around the crowd with a stack of business cards in hand and it's very obvious their goal is to get those cards in as many hands as possible. If they interrupt you and me while we're having a private but very beneficial networking conversation, that doesn't bother them at all. They may at least say "Excuse me, I just wanted to give you one of these …", but the net result is at best we couldn't care less. At worst, they just became branded as the kind of networking professional you and I don't want anything to do with.

In their defense, they may simply not know any better. They may not have made a professional study of the great game of networking like you, and they may have a boss who hasn't either and has mandated that they "Be sure they don't come back to the office until they've given out all their business cards!" Whatever may be the reason, the result is a sad case study in the exact WRONG way to play the great game of networking.

What do you suppose happens to cards we receive under those circumstances? When I ask that in my seminars, several audience members usually make a gesture like they're tearing a card up and/or throwing imaginary versions of those cards in the trash, and as I tell the audience, that is correct! I usually add that throwing it away is the most *polite* thing I've ever done with a card I received in that way!

Do you see why, as a professional networker, I find that action so very offensive?

Right! It's offensive because that person obviously doesn't care about you or me. They care about themselves. They care about their own goals and agendas, and that is not the kind of person with whom you and I want to network.

Now, as you play the great game of networking, you will have the opportunity to not only hand out your own business cards, but to exchange them with professionals like yourself who are as eager to get them as you are to hand them out. In a few pages we'll see how to properly facilitate this exchange, but for now and for the sake of your future as a professional in this great game, remember that handing out business cards by itself is not networking! Before you get out of the car at networking events, close your eyes, grip the steering wheel tightly and whisper firmly, "I am not here just to hand out business cards!" Good for you!

#2: You Are the Brand

Networking can take place virtually anywhere, as we've discussed. Networking is a key component of branding. Anything and everything you do is part of your brand, and you can also be sending "branding" messages anywhere, good or bad, so remember that as you go about playing the great game of networking. Remember you're always being judged, evaluated, and tested, so you want to be sure you're at your best.

As such, you don't want to be cutting people off for parking spaces at networking events, you don't want to be rude to the wait staff, you don't want to be the person telling the dirtiest jokes, and you don't want to be first in line at the buffet. When they announce the bar has opened, you don't want to holler, "Yee-ha," run over and challenge the room to a drinking game. You get the idea.

I'm obviously exaggerating, but think about how your enthusiasm for referring, or doing business with people in your network, could quickly dim if you see them acting in a manner that is inconsistent with that of a professional. I have seen this happen too many times to even be funny any more. You are the brand, and everything you do is branding!

Roughly 55% of how people perceive us is based on how we act, or our body language. About 38% is based on the tonality or how we say what we say, and 7% of how we are perceived is based on the actual words we use. You have probably seen these statistics. They're from a study conducted in 1967 by Albert Mehrabian, Ph.D., of the University of California, Los Angeles (UCLA). Though the original studies have been replicated often, the numbers haven't wavered that much. What this tells us is that we need to not only have our "talk" down, we need to "walk our talk" in everything we do because the impressions others have of us depend largely on our actions.

As you're out playing the great game of networking, make note of the actions of the people you see around you. You'll probably find that even if you hadn't consciously paid that much attention to the actions of others in the past, those actions have impacted how you perceived the person and his or her professionalism.

That's enough about what not to do. Let's get back to being positive and talk now about some of things you CAN and SHOULD do to effectively build your personal brand.

Appearance

I believe a person should dress as well as they should, and as well as is appropriate for his or her industry. This may be something you want to research for your particular profession, and I also don't want you to feel like you have to do what everyone else does. That's why I recommend you dress as well as you *should*. If you're a securities broker who hopes to earn my retirement account or that of my aging parents, that probably means wearing a suit or at least a coat & tie most of the time at events you attend. If you're a lawn care service or a siding company, however, wearing a suit may seem inappropriate, if not downright ridiculous! If you over-dressed in that situation, people might perceive that you're a higher-caliber, very successful professional, or they may think you're too dainty to do any work! So again, I'd suggest you do your own research regarding what is appropriate.

Something I've seen done very effectively is logo wear. It is very cost effective to have your logo or just your company name put on a shirt or jacket, and it literally gives your organization a "uniform" look. This can give you and your team a very sharp look and can help reinforce your brand in a very positive way. A polo shirt with khakis or dress pants, for example, can be a very crisp and professional look for just about any occupation or industry.

The other thing that will influence your decisions on how to dress are obviously the standards of the events you attend. A good rule is to dress your very best when attending for the first time. It's better to jokingly apologize for being over-dressed than to stick out like a sore thumb by showing up at a "business attire" event in a t-shirt! If you're ever in doubt regarding what is appropriate, contact the people putting on the event and ask them. You can tell them what you plan to wear and let them tell you if it's appropriate.

Exactly what constitutes "business attire," or even "appropriate dress," has really been debated over the past few years, so expect that to continue in the future. I wish I had the definitive answer, but I don't, so I strongly urge you to contact the host of the event or people you trust who are familiar with the event and obtain guidance from them.

The Food

This may seem so basic and so obvious that it shouldn't even be mentioned, but our relationship with food is something of which we need to be very mindful at networking events! First, we don't want to be the first in the buffet line every time! I actually know someone who does this, and sadly, it's a running joke at meetings. The announcement of the opening of the buffet is like a starter gun to this guy, and he makes a bee line for it! Once, when this happened, a colleague of mine said, "Boy, you sure don't wanna get between him and the trough!" Many of us don't want to refer business to the person who attends a networking event just to eat, either. We're not going to be too eager to give our business or a referral to someone who acts more interested in the food than in those of us with whom he or she could network.

It may be an honest mistake, but let's honestly try not to make it! Many networking events are held at lunch and many of us are too busy to have breakfast, so when we get a chance to eat, boy, we want to eat! We just need to be mindful of how that may look to the people who eat with us, and be sure we practice our manners. If you have any doubt about the right and wrong way to dine, take an inexpensive course, or read a book on the subject. You'll find you have a lot more confidence, and just feel better about yourself, when you know you are well-mannered in a dining situation.

How We Act

Be nice! There will probably be a line to check in at most events. Accept this not as a major bummer, but as a great networking opportunity to have a conversation with those in line around you. Your brand will not be enhanced by your standing in line with your arms folded and a scowl on your face! Be nice to those putting on the event and to the wait staff. I read an article about a leader who takes job candidates to lunch as part of the interview process, to observe how they treat the wait staff. If the candidate is rude or condescending to the wait staff, it can reveal things about that candidate's true character and the leader will rarely extend an offer to that candidate, regardless of his or her qualifications. The better you treat everyone around you, (including competitors!), the better your brand will flourish. You never know who may be watching.

It's also important to remember we are making impressions all the time when interacting with people. I have heard others share stories, and I have my own, about people who act one way when they're doing what they think is "networking," but are different other times. Driving aggressively in the parking lot at an event (I have even heard of people cutting one another off for a parking space at the same event they are attending!), telling jokes or stories that could be considered offensive, casually flicking cigarette butts, or merely the fact that they smoke, are among things that can damage the otherwise positive impression a member of a network has. Trust me, I've seen it happen, and you do not want to be in the unfortunate position of trying to change a negative impression. Give thought to not only how you act at the event, but at any interaction you have with people with whom you network, or in any situation in which you might be observed. You'll benefit not only from your improved image within your network, but you'll brighten the day of some folks who will really appreciate the attention from a professional like you. When you see these kinds of reactions, you'll benefit too!

So that we don't end this section on a sour note, here's a story of how gracious behavior can build a brand. A few years ago, at an American Marketing Association luncheon, were two competitors, both of whom happened to be friends of mine. One was the meeting sponsor that day, which meant she had the opportunity to put business cards and promotional materials at the place of each attendee. She was running a little late, and my other friend, who was a direct competitor and also a member of the group, jumped in and helped her place her materials on the tables. These two folks are always professional and, as far as I know, always gracious to one another in situations like this. But, when one took the initiative to help the other get the most benefit from her sponsorship, that really impressed me. So much so, that I've tried to tell the story as often as I can. If it's a local engagement I mention the name of the person who did the helping. Again, I always liked him, but he made me a proud bearer of the standard that presents the flag of his brand by going the extra mile. How you act is always being evaluated, and even judged. Think "big picture," and "long term," about the kind of stories you want others telling about you!

Alcohol

I am very often asked how one's relationship with alcohol should be handled when playing the great game of networking. My suggestion is to avoid drinking alcohol at these events altogether. You never know who might be offended by the fact that you drink, for whatever reason, and my belief is that you're better off not creating that hurdle for yourself as you play the great game of networking. Granted, there are some who claim they wouldn't do business with anyone who wouldn't join them in a drink, but I don't think I'd bet my future on that.

Lest you think I'm being overly uptight or judgmental, I might add that for a few years when I was younger, I was a social drinker (with more emphasis on "drinker" than "social," I report shamefully!"). I still have many friends who drink at various competitive levels, and I don't hold it against them, but the ironic thing is I've also heard them share stories about how they lost respect for those around them who, in a networking situation, had what they considered to be "a few too many," suggesting this is a sword that can cut both ways.

So, I first suggest you don't do it at all, or if you do, be mindful of your behavior and how you could be perceived with a drink in your hand.

For specific guidance on how to act in business and social situations of all kind, I recommend books in the Emily Post series. Though Mrs. Post passed away several years ago, and the company is now run by her grandchildren, her principles have stood the test of time. You'll find some of the newer books address things like cell phone use, and other social no-no's you'll want to avoid, along with some great ways to distinguish yourself through your manners. I'm often amazed at what a powerful impression a polite, well-mannered person makes, and how far that goes toward brand building. It's kind of sad that such behavior is the exception rather than the norm, but it's also encouraging to know that your professional, well-mannered behavior is almost guaranteed to pay off for you. I can guarantee good manners will never hurt you.

Egad, that voice!

Pay close attention to your tonality. It's one of those things that can impact how others perceive you and your brand. Try to speak loud enough to be heard, and certainly speak with confidence, but don't overpower people with your voice. If the person is wincing, it probably means you're talking too loud. That booming, commanding voice may sound great to you, or be quite moving in the choir on Sunday, but put yourself in the shoes (or ears) of the listener. If the impression they get of you is a headache, that's not the brand we want. Sometimes we talk loudly and don't realize it because we're nervous or just aren't aware of how we sound, but pay close attention to this. Conversely, we don't want to have a mousy, mumbling, murmuring tonality. If the listener keeps having to lean in to hear us or if they keep saying "Hmm?",

"What?", or "Huh?," you probably need to speak up, project, slow down, or just be more clear.

On the other hand, once you've developed rapport, you can use voice inflection to really drive home your point. Here's an example of one of the attention-getters I used in promoting my marketing research services. When asked what I did, I'd lean in and respond in a fairly hushed tone, barely above a whisper, "I can tell you things about your customers ..." like it was secret, super-sensitive, information. It caught the listener's attention and they wanted to know more. I went back into regular tone for the rest of the conversation. You'll of course want to experiment with what works best for your message, the situation, etc. The key thing is to make tonality work for your personal brand. Making sure you have a breath mint before you start networking is a good idea, too.

#3: Be Confident, But Don't be Arrogant!

People love to be around confident people like you! The confidence you exude not only gives them a secure feeling about your brand, but is also contagious in a way they really appreciate. Confident people are eagerly added to the networks of those who can be of help to them, and are confidently referred to members of their networks. Be confident! Maybe even a little bold ...

... But don't be arrogant! It's good to be confident about our product and how it can change people's lives, but it's not good to come across like the best thing since pickle loaf. Confident people are eagerly accepted, but arrogant people are eagerly and summarily dismissed. You'll see people like this at events, so watch and learn from their poor example. Use them as a benchmark for how not to act in any networking situation, or any other situation involving relationship building. Dr. Denis Waitley said in *The Psychology of Winning*, "Arrogance is God's gift to shallow people", and whether people are familiar with that quote or not, they are familiar with the feeling relegated to those who have the gift (more like *curse!*) of arrogance.

Once you finish this book you will have the tools to enable you to confidently network. The more effort you make to apply them, the more confident you'll get and your success in and out of official networking arenas will grow exponentially. You'll also find several books from a variety of authors on my website which can help empower you in many areas. I share that suggestion with you because if you've picked up this book, you probably make a habit of reading and listening to audio books as often as you can, so if you're not familiar with some of these you may want to check them out. If there's an area you'd like to study but don't see on my booklist or don't hear mentioned in this book, drop me an e-mail at www.burtmarketing.com and I'll see if I can offer you some direction.

The best thing you can do to become more confident, however, is not only to read and broaden that spectacular mind of yours, but to make a point of taking ACTION! Just reading another book is a good thing, but it's not really an ACTION and that means your investment of your time and money will not pay off as much as you and I both know you'd like. Many times we avoid trying new things or stretching our comfort zones because we fear failure. If you want to succeed at networking or anything else, you've got to change your vocabulary starting right now. There are no failures, there are only outcomes. You'll gain confidence by building on those outcomes that netted you the results you wanted, and by viewing any that don't, using them as superb research to help you do better the next time.

Another very important thing is to visualize not only taking the action, but succeeding. See yourself making good relationships and getting the outcomes you desire. See yourself effortlessly opening conversations and opening relationships. See yourself as the person in the room that the person you're talking too wants to meet more than anyone else. Imagine in detail the great debt of gratitude the other person will convey to you once you open that relationship and help them. Experience the emotions associated with success beforehand. See yourself enjoying every minute of your play in the great game of networking. Your subconscious mind will plot the course for you if you dial in the right coordinates.

Do. Or do not. There is no try.—Yoda

#4: Take the Initiative

Taking the initiative is a personal demonstration of your confidence. It shows the other person he or she is important enough to warrant your interest, and that you have the courage to introduce yourself to a total stranger.

Some specific and powerfully simple ways to confidently take the initiative are:

1. Giving a firm, but not lethal, handshake

2. Making eye contact

3. Stating your name first

Firm, but not Lethal, Handshake

Networking events are literally opportunities to "press flesh." The handshake is a time—honored ritual business professionals use to open and close every encounter. Don't be shy about engaging in the handshake. Squeeze the other person's hand "firmly," but don't try to crush their hand! That makes an enemy out of the person receiving the handshake, and makes the person with the iron grip look like a big jerk. In fact, an overly-firm handshake is believed by some to convey insecurity. Be firm enough to demonstrate you are a solid person, but don't hurt anybody! Of course, a timid little half-handshake or a flabby, mushy handshake is a brand-killer too. There are lots of places to research the do's and don'ts of the handshake, but the best thing you can do is find some willing volunteers, of various age and gender, and get them to help you "practice" your handshake.

Make Eye Contact

I advise you make a point of looking the other person in the eye, particularly when you meet them. This is an important part of the "brand *you*" package. This shows you have the confidence to face the people you meet. Not making eye contact can not only convey insecurity, or suggest you're not worthy to enter into a relationship with the person to whom you're speaking, it could result in a violation of Principle #1. You might be misinterpreted as arrogant! Remember, people gravitate to confident people, and will avoid arrogant people. I recall, at a meeting some time ago, a friend of mine in the research business introduced me to a student who had worked as an intern for him and wanted to meet me, to see if I could help him find a job. The young man greeted me with a very soggy handshake, (strike one!), and as he did so, he sort of looked off to the side and down, wearing an expression I would categorize somewhere between a scowl and a frown (steeeriiiiike twooooooo!). I really don't recall if or what we talked about, because I mostly tuned out after that. Like most people, I don't have a need for arrogant people in my network. The first chance I got, I told the friend who introduced us that there was no way I was going to work with someone that arrogant. The friend profusely apologized and clamored to explain. He practically begged me not to hold it against the student because he was not at all arrogant, but was incredibly, painfully, cripplingly shy. Well, that was a different story. As a shy person myself I could certainly empathize. I really wanted to be in his corner. I told my friend to have the student send me a resume. I wish I could tell you this story has a happy ending. I would have been happy to work with and coach the student, and to have even helped him find employment, but the cover letter he sent had 17 spelling and grammatical errors! Seventeen! Steeeeriiiiike, thu-reeeeeee!

It's not a staring contest, but you need to make enough eye contact to acknowledge the other person, and let him or her know they are important to you. Some books advocate letting them set the pace for how much eye contact you should make once the conversation gets going, and that's usually what I try to do. Just be confident enough to look the other person in the eye.

State your Own Name First

"Hi, Burt Smith," or "Hi, I'm Burt." It's as simple as that. You convey a great deal of confidence in yourself by volunteering your own name first. If they don't volunteer their name right away, I'll ask. This technique is good for both in-person meetings, and when connecting over the phone. Like much of what I'm suggesting in the book, though, I encourage you to try this yourself and observe your results.

A Word of Caution

While I strongly believe the techniques discussed in the above section are valid, and I'm confident they will help you make the best possible impression, I must also point out that all my networking takes place in the United States, and primarily in the Southwestern and Midwestern regions. When visiting different regions of the country, different cultures, and different parts of the world, brush up on the customs. Know beforehand what is acceptable and what isn't. The last thing you want to do is insult potential members of your network.

You probably knew that already. I say that because I learned it when a seminar participant came up to me after a workshop and very politely and sincerely schooled me on how making eye contact in some cultures is a great insult. He used the specific example of the Native American culture, which really got my attention since I'm from Oklahoma and have a Native American heritage myself. So, know your culture.

#5: Take the Focus Off Yourself!

A sure way to be a hit at any event, and to help your own confidence level, is to make a point of taking the focus off yourself, which is precisely why that's Guiding Principle Number 5 in the great game of networking. Much of our apprehension in unfamiliar situations comes because we're just sure everyone is looking at us, knows what we're thinking, and is thinking the worst about us. It's simply not true. The fact is, other people at most networking events aren't thinking about you, they're thinking the same thing you are. They may be so nervous, they're just hoping to get out of there alive! Seriously, we need to remember that most people's natural tendency is to focus on themselves. We should use that knowledge to not only feel more confident in networking situations, but should turn that piece of knowledge to our advantage. If what they want to think of most is himself or herself, let them! Indulge them! Encourage them! Make that *your* focus too, and you'll be amazed how popular you quickly become.

A Dale Carnegie's Human Relations Principles says, "Make the other person feel important." One way to very effectively do this was discussed in a previous principle in which we learned the importance of being a good listener. Get the other person talking, listen intently, and remind yourself to take the focus off yourself and put it on your fellow networkers, where it belongs. Meeting people and making friends are your goal. Think about it, and say it to yourself before, during, and after every networking event. In the Advanced Networking section, we'll look at some specific ways our follow up can help reinforce these points.

The Magic Words ...

A question you may have is, "What do I say?", when determining how to open a conversation with someone you've just met. Here's a sure-fire winner. You'll be astounded at how this works. Simply say,

Tell me about your business ...

Or

Tell me what you do ...

Some of my networking colleagues like to ask, "Who's a prospect for you?", so they can learn all about the specific target market the person serves and how to best help them. That works for them, and will probably work for you too, but I just like simply saying "Tell me about your business" and that opens a conversation that can be taken in a lot of different directions. The real key, though, is to make sure our focus is on the other person and that we make them the star.

Remember, the better you treat the other person, and the more important they feel, the higher the regard in which they will hold you. That high regard *will* translate into more introductions, positive word of mouth, and ultimately the reaching of your goals through the help of others. There are people out there willing to be champions for you and your cause; they're just waiting for you to give them a good reason to be.

#6: Look for Strangers and be Their Ambassador

Here's a way to quickly make a whole bunch of friends and build your personal brand in the process. Look for strangers and be their personal ambassador! If you see someone you don't know, introduce yourself! Ask them if they come here quite a bit and you can start a conversation from there. If this is their first time and your first time, you've just met a great buddy with whom you can learn together. If they've been here before and you haven't, they'll be a great source of information. If you've been here before and they haven't, you may make a great friend by being the person who helps them have a good experience coming here.

An important thing to remember is that most of us are pushed a little outside our comfort zone when we attend an event like a luncheon, or an event designed especially for networking. Meeting "new people," and doing so in a "new environment," can be a little taxing. How very beneficial it is if there's at least one person who helps make that a good experience, and how very valuable it is to you if you are that person.

Actively seek opportunities to find "strangers," and be their ambassador.

This whole ambassador idea came to me after having served as an official ambassador in some of the organizations where I was a member. Typically, every organization has an ambassador committee, or a welcome wagon committee, or some group whose job it is to make sure attendees have a good experience. We'll talk more about how you can really make this work for you in an official capacity in a later section, but there's a lot of potential value for you in acting as an "unofficial" ambassador, too. Remember, you are the brand, and you represent your profession. You want to be sure you stand out, and do so in a positive way, and the most positive way is to look for others you can help. So what I do, and encourage you to do too, is to give yourself a little promotion at any event you attend, and become an ambassador. If you see someone you don't know, introduce yourself. If they seem to need help with something, offer to help. If they have a question, simply say, "I don't know, but I'll find out." Even if your response is "I don't know, this is actually my first time here, but I'll sure see if I can help you …", you'll endear yourself to that person. Imagine how you would react if someone who is here for the first time, not associated with the organization in any way, wants to help you for no other apparent reason than they want to be of help to you. They will be incredibly impressed with your service ethic and will want to know what you do. They'll be taken aback by how helpful you are offering to be and will associate that helpfulness with excellent service and a powerful brand. The brand that is YOU! This will also help you quickly show up on the radar of the organization you're visiting. You're helping them build their brand and they will appreciate it. They'll want to know who you are and what you do, and that could quickly put you in a position to be involved in leadership in the organization and send you business. I urge you to try this not just because you will quickly see your brand value escalate, but because helping others is part of the FUN of playing the great game of networking.

"A stranger is just a friend you haven't met yet."—Uncle Jessie, from an episode of the Dukes of Hazzard

#7: Get Them Talking, and LET THEM TALK!

This principle is often the one my workshop attendees tell me helps them the most. It's so incredibly simple! It's powerful because of its simplicity. People will think you are brilliant for using it because so very few people engaged in "conversations" actually do. It will work for you, it will profit you, and you will want to thank me profusely for sharing it with you. But before I do, I have to tell you, I didn't come up with the idea myself. I learned it from studying the lessons of Dale Carnegie. He wrote a book that remains a bestseller today: *How to Win Friends and Influence People*. This book is required reading for networking and business success! And I'm not just saying that because I used to be a Dale Carnegie Instructor. This book helped me long before I ever even took a Dale Carnegie course. In fact, I had people telling me about how beneficial it was long before I had sense enough to sit down and read it. It can do the same for you.

Dale Carnegie started out as an extremely shy farm boy from Missouri who spent his life studying how to be more confident, and helped others by sharing what he learned. In his book, Mr. Carnegie gives us a set of human relations principles on how to build rapport with, and influence others, and most of it boils down to being a good listener and having respect for the other person. Simple but powerful, it can be read in a day. I encourage you to pick up a copy. If you've already read it, pick it up again to see what other gems you can find!

Get them talking … and let them talk!

Getting people talking is really easy enough because, as said previously, people generally are most focused on themselves. Because this is a networking event we are attending for the purpose typically of opening business relationships, what we hear from them in our initial conversation will help us frame the conversation from that point forward. We will learn more about what that person is all about, what their business needs are, and we can then respond with how our product can make their lives better. So a good rule of thumb is to not only get the other person talking, but be sure we follow Dale Carnegie's admonition, to be a good listener. You may think you're already a good listener, and I hope so, but my guess is that you and I could both stand to improve ourselves in this area. Often we are very good at opening the conversation with questions about what the other person does, and they give us a good response, then we launch into how what we do can be of benefit to them, yak, yak, yak, blah, blah, blah. Our hearts are in the right place and our intentions are good, they really are, but there's a much better way to build rapport. Get the other person talking, but make sure you take full interest in them, and *let them talk!* Let them tell you all about what's important to them. Interact only with questions showing interest in what they are saying.

When they finally do stop talking, your relationship will go to an entirely new level. Even if the person speaking is the most self-absorbed, egotistical person you've ever met, they won't be able to talk forever. They'll share and share and share, then eventually the conversation has to turn to you, and that will beg from them the inevitable question, "What do you do?" You've just spent the last few minutes demonstrating what a patient, caring person you are. Imagine what a receptive audience you'll have! When you do respond, you can tailor what you're saying to the things you've learned are important to them. Give this amazing technique a try. And be prepared to be amazed at how well it works.

Here's a little tip you may find helpful, too. I had a very good sales manager years ago who helped me become a better listener. Like a lot of eager sales people, I was always in a hurry to share how my product was the solution to their problem; to take the floor and "present." Even though my enthusiasm was commendable, if I do say so myself, this tended to rub the prospective client the wrong way. That action suggested that I was a person who was merely waiting to talk, not a patient, professional, active listener. My sales manager suggested that after I asked a question, I should gently bite down on the tip of my tongue. I started doing that, exerting just enough pressure to remind me to keep my yap shut until the other person was ready to listen, and it made a huge difference. Give that one a try, and get ready to go to the bank!

EXERCISE: Pay special attention over the next few days to conversations in which you're involved. Note how many people don't really listen, but merely wait to talk. Notice how often their contributions to the conversation are, in the vast majority of instances, about themselves, even if it doesn't seem exactly relevant. They just seem to have this great desire to talk, and mostly about themselves. They probably don't mean anything by it, but as you pay more attention, notice how some participants in a conversation with a person like this could be mildly offended. At the very least, you may observe that the other party to the conversation will quickly realize that they are not the primary focus of the conversation. In <u>The Seven Habits of Highly Effective People</u>, Dr. Steven Covey called this "Monologues in duet."

It goes without saying, we should also pay attention to our own contributions to "conversations," and make sure we're actively listening, not just waiting to talk ourselves!

If this hurts, it means you did it right!

#8: Never Sit With Someone You Know!

This one is more a commandment than a guiding principle! This one helps you be more successful in the great game of networking and helps ensure you don't take opportunities away from those in your networking group.

If you go to a networking function and spend the majority of your time with people you know, you are not only depriving yourself of the opportunity to meet new acquaintances and grow both your network and your bank account. You are also depriving the members of your network from doing that too! Think about it. If you two already know one another and are any kind of professional player in the great game of networking at all, you already know who one another is, who a prospect is for one another, and how to help one another. To spend additional time at an event at which you could both add to your networks is hurting you both! You are, in essence, taking money out of one another's pockets! So stop it!

It's awfully easy to fall into the trap of spending time at such events only with people we know. This is not just a comfort-zone issue, it's because we probably have found we really enjoy the company of these folks. That's great, but it's also highly counterproductive to the great game of networking for all involved. Please raise your hand and repeat after me.

> *I vow with all my heart and at the risk of never being allowed in the arena to play the great game of networking again that I shall never, never, never, ever, ever sit with someone I know at a networking event. Ever! So help me Burt.*

Thank you. You just made a commitment that will keep your network growing and producing revenue for you like an oil well! Never, ever sit with someone you know!

#8a.... except under certain circumstances.

With every rule comes an exception, so let's make sure we keep the rule of exceptions alive and well here. Obviously, if you are attending an event with a guest, someone you already know and invited, it would be very bad etiquette to abandon them at the door. "Ok, meet you back here at 1:15, gotta go build my network and you do too, so good luck. Meet lots of people! Enjoy!" That would be inappropriate, to say the least. If you have a guest with you, your brand may then be judged on how gracious a host you are, so that's where you'll want to spend most of your energy. Introduce your guest around, make taking care of them and helping them have a good experience your focus, and just do right by them. You'll probably wind up meeting and introducing your guest to several new folks that day, too, so your time will pay off not only in how well you take care of your guest and build that relationship, but from the other ways things just seem to happen magically in the great game of networking.

Another time I've found myself breaking this important rule is when there are clients, or key members of my network, who are at an event with whom I don't get to spend the kind of time I'd like. As members of my network, I certainly should be able to simply call them up and get some time to visit with them if need be, or to schedule a lunch with them because we both know the time spent would be profitable. But life being life, and success being success, that sometimes becomes easier said than done, and I expect you'll experience this too. It may turn out that a networking event, Chamber of Commerce luncheon, association meeting, or whatever, may be among the few or only times you get to see certain members of your network. If your gut tells you to spend that lunch sitting with that member of your network, then go for it. The rule is in place to make sure you both safeguard your most precious resource, your time, but time invested in one another should be valuable and enjoyable too.

#9: It's Your Party, and Everyone's Invited!

Remember, the underlying fundamental principle of the great game of networking is helping others. The other is about having a ball doing it, of course! Our careers consist of being champions for products, or causes, that we believe will better the lives of others, so we strive to meet and share these products with as many people as possible. We know people will be more receptive to learning more about our products if they feel good about us, because we know that they don't separate our brand from our person. To them, we're one and the same. We know that anywhere we are and anything we do is a component part of the overall machine that is our brand. And we know the simplest, best way to build positive impressions is to commit to helping others as often as we can. This is why we open doors for folks at networking events, offer to help the speaker carry in their materials, or even offer to pour a refill of water for the folks sitting on either side of us at a networking luncheon. Because a service attitude is part of who we are! It's our *brand!*

For doing these things and for being professional in all things we do, we build a network of professionals who may buy from us and will confidently refer us to others who can benefit from what we have to offer. We should also look for opportunities to do the same for them.

A wonderful benefit of playing the great game of networking is participating in win-win relationships. Yes, we of course hope to get business and referrals from our fellow networkers, and it's especially gratifying to be able to help them too.

For starters, we should keep our fellow networkers in mind at all times so they'll do the same for you. When at an event, remember to be an ambassador like we talked about a few pages back. If you're in a conversation with someone and someone else you happen to know walks up, invite them into the conversation! Be an ambassador. Make an introduction. A good way to do this is by asking a question as you greet the person. "Hello Sue, glad you could make it today. Sue, do you know Frank? Frank and I were just visiting about ..." Notice I used both parties' names twice. This helps everyone get more familiar with everyone's names. It's also a good idea to introduce the introduction with a question. That way you don't waste even a second of your precious time on the clock of the great game of networking attempting to introduce people who already know one another.

As your relationships grow, helping your fellow networkers by sending them business is also important, though sometimes tricky, so we'll talk about that a few pages down.

In the mean time, always make yourself the host and work to help your fellow networkers however you can. If there's someone you meet that you feel they should meet, help the two meet! A good state of mind I like to put myself into is to think of networking as a party. My party, your party, and to act like everyone is invited! Each networking "party" you attend is bigger (or potentially bigger) than the one before.

Assume the role of benevolent host and navigate the room meeting new friends, greeting old ones, and helping anyone who hasn't yet become connected become connected. This will give attendees the rightful impression that you not only play the great game of networking, but you ARE the great game of networking. This is the spot you want to be in when people think about the product or service you have to offer, and it's the exact spot in which you want any of your competitors to perceive you. See why I like to call it the great game of networking? Isn't this fun?

#10: Never Leave a Conversation Empty Handed!

So you've tooled up to play the great game of networking. You've worked the room, met several interesting prospects, had a chance to share your marketing statement, and have been the benevolent host of the most exciting networking party to date. All of this can be for naught if we don't have an important component part in our networking machine: the ability to contact those we meet. Thus we conclude the principles with the single most important action you take in opening networking relationships: Making sure you get business cards of the people you meet!

Like most of what we've talked about so far, this is very simple, but so simple we sometimes forget to do it, so we're concluding this section by stressing how you should end every conversation you have with any prospective new member of your professional network: Never leave that conversation empty handed! Get the other person's business card!

There is a simple way to do this. Just conclude every conversation by reaching for your card and asking, "Could I have one of your cards?"

What are they going to say? "No, sorry, I just had these printed and if I give you one I'll only have 499 left and I hate to break up a set"? Business cards are the tools of the trade. They must have your card, and you must have theirs, to help make the networking magic work. So simply ask, non-threateningly, every time you conclude a conversation, "Could I have one of your cards?"

What if they don't have a card with them? Sadly, everyone may not take the great game of networking as seriously as you, and some may have forgotten their cards, or may be so new they don't have theirs printed yet, or who knows what. If they don't have a card with them, make sure they get your card. Then, take our one of the other cards you collected that day or some scratch paper and jot down their contact information. At the very least, get their company name and mailing address. If you can also get their website, phone, and e-mail, that's great too, but rather than spend too much time, having their company name & address should be enough to enable you to do an internet search and get the rest and add them to your contact database. We'll talk about making effective use of your contact database in a later section, but for now, be sure you never leave a conversation empty handed. Get a business card!

5

After the Event

After the Event

We've talked about playing the great game of networking, and how to "do networking" at various venues. Many people think that's what "networking" is, and they are sadly mistaken. Their loss is your gain, however, because the great game of networking only begins with the initial contact. Except for a few rare cases, the real value and payoff for networking takes place in the tremendously important post-event activities. Here are some principles to guide us after we've attended the event.

Following Up Is As Important As Showing Up

Woody Allen said "70% of success is showing up." And he was at least half right! Unless we actively go out and seek our destiny, the likelihood of it finding us is pretty remote. As well it should be! A go-getter like you yearns for a challenge, so why should you be deprived of it? Yes, it takes work to be successful, but that makes the accomplishment that much more enjoyable. Just getting out there and "showing up" takes courage. Pushing yourself to enter what may be a room full of strangers and introduce yourself takes shear guts, and you deserve the respect you have earned from me and a host of others who undoubtedly have great admiration for your ability to play the great game of networking.

But the great game of networking only begins with the introduction. Many just don't get this, and their incomes show it. They think networking is basically "visiting," on company time. Go to an event, meet some people, collect some business cards, then go back to doing whatever. These next few sections show you how to make your investment in the networking event pay off for you many times over. Please raise your right hand and repeat loudly:

I fully understand, as a professional, all star player in the great game of networking, the game does not end with the close of the event or even with my obtaining a business card. It has only begun, just as the incredible amount of success I seek for myself has only begun. And I wouldn't have it any other way, because getting to play the great game of networking is a privilege, not a right, and I vow to play it so well, the next book about networking will be written either by me or about me. So help me Burt.

So, anyhow, following up is as important as showing up. Now that you have the business cards of some people you've met, it's time to do the thing that can really, really build your personal brand with them. Time to do something most amateurs who don't really belong in the great game of networking hate to do, but something real professional players in the great game of networking cheerfully do because they know the power derived from its action. And yet again, it's powerful in its simplicity.

I'm speaking about the writing and sending of a hand-written note. Send these babies to people you meet at networking events and your brand will be elevated. Make it a point to send hand-written thank you notes to new acquaintances made in the great game of networking, or anyone else you just want to "touch," and you'll be amazed what that will do for you.

Here's why. For one thing, most of us who get personal notes are impressed because we know how much trouble it is to write them. Most of the professionals I know make a practice of sending out personal notes, and none of us are as good at doing it as we'd like to be. Regardless of how many we send, it seems we'd always like to send more, so when we get one in the mail, we have great appreciation for the gesture. This is something you definitely want to do!

Some evidence that drove home the importance of the hand-written thank-you note came from my friend Mike Newcombe, who is a fellow past-president of the American Marketing Association. He said he really appreciates getting a thank you note, because he knows all too well how hard they are to write! Indeed! I thought about it and I felt the same way, and it's probable you or anyone you send these to will experience a similar appreciation. People know these require additional time, effort, energy and creativity, and those are the kinds of words you want them associating with your brand. Just so you'll know, I wrote

Mike a thank-you note right after I wrote this paragraph and I'll thank him again here in the book. *Thanks, Mike*!

Despite several technologically advanced alternatives available today, I contend these notes have to be hand written to have the most effect. There are a number of software programs that enable you to do mail merges, print labels, print envelopes, etc. The time these will save you will be worth nowhere near the brand equity you can gain with the recipient. You'll learn more in the section on database usage. There is a new service a colleague of mine told me about that gets a handwriting sample from you and replicates a font to match it. They then let you send out customized cards to anyone in your database and they even use first class postage. Basically you just go in and type a short note, select the address to which you want your card sent, and it shows up in their mailbox in a day or two, saving you writer's cramp and a trip to the post office. I haven't tried this but I do believe it has potential. E-mail me and I'll gladly share a link where you can check this out for yourself and even ask someone who is using it what they think. I must say I do believe this will be something that will benefit you, but since I haven't tried it myself I am reluctant to fully endorse it just now. But keep an eye out at www.burtmarketing.com to see if that changes.

Here's a little scenario to illustrate why I'm so sold on the handwritten personal note. Imagine you've been to a networking event and made a connection you really like. It's a couple of days later and the person you met is going through her mail. She probably sorts it like the rest of us, "Bill, bill, junk mail, bill … wait a second, what's this?" she says as she discovers your card. "My name, hand written … hmm." She opens the card and reads,

Sue,

Thanks for the opportunity to visit with you at the Chamber of Commerce luncheon the other day. Congratulations on the positive momentum you have going for you at the XYZ corporation. I hope when we see

one another at a future event I'll get to hear an update on the next exciting thing you're up to! Take care!

Chances are she'll say, "Wow. How impressive! I just met this person, and here they are following up with me. How sincere," or something to that effect. Because it's unique in that it's hand written, your note gets opened first so you're not lost in the shuffle with the junk mail, or bills, and as such, you're disassociated with the bad news and associated with a positive event, one you created, in fact, which is where you want to be.

What tends to occur is that no matter how solid a first impression we've made, once the nice folks we meet get back into their worlds, their minds are back on their own survival or success, and we may get pushed to the background. A personal note can help bring us back to the foreground and will reinforce the positive impression they had of us. They may forget the other 15 people they met that day, but by sending a personal note we just put ourselves into a whole new category of professionalism in their eyes.

If this person, or his or her organization, has a sales force, they wish their sales people would do these kinds of gestures to help build the brand of their organization. Don't be surprised if you later learn they take your note and make it the topic of the next meeting. They may wave it in front of their employees and ask, "Why can't you people do things like this for our clients?"

This simple little solution also addresses the concern some of my peers raise about using the backs of their business cards as a mini-brochure instead of leaving it blank. Recall that some of my colleagues do this so people they give it to can use the blank space on the back to take notes regarding the conversation they have when they initially meet. Sending a personal, handwritten note makes it unnecessary to put the burden on the person you meet to take notes to remind them who you are. Your note does that very powerfully for you.

Your note may also make their day! You never know what is going on in someone's world. Maybe they're feeling overworked, maybe they don't feel so appreciated, maybe their personal life isn't quite where they'd like it to be, or maybe they just need *somebody* to give them a little lift. Your card, simple as it may be, could do just that. In any case, you will see positive returns for the writing of a personal note. I could tell you I know this from experience, but I'd rather you try it and experience this for yourself!

We also want to be sure to include a business card. This probably sounds redundant or perhaps even pointless considering that I suggested only a few pages ago the importance of ending every networking conversation and thus opening every networking relationship by exchanging business cards. So you wonder why on earth would I advocate enclosing a second business card? Let's once again visit the world of this new acquaintance ...

We met these nice people at a networking event. We engaged them in conversation, we let them talk, and talk, and talk, interjecting only to ask questions about THEM. You had a great moment together, they remarked on what a privilege it was to meet a professional of your caliber and they eagerly took your business card while handing you one of theirs. They then rushed back to their office. They snatched their favorite frame off their desk and ripped out whatever was in it and replaced it with your business card. They then, in one dramatic, sweeping motion, raked their family pictures off the corner of their desk and put the frame that now contained your card in that spot. They then lit a few candles and placed them all around your card to give notice to the world the awesome stature in which you are held.

That being the case, if they ever had the chance to refer any business our way, there is no way they would part with that sacred card, so we need to send them another one so they can give it away.

It could happen.

On the other hand, what is slightly more likely is that despite all their good intentions, they have misplaced your business card. Or, Heaven forbid, they met a bunch of other people that day and may have mistaken you for someone else. Getting a new card helps make sure they know who you are and how to contact you. Always include a business card with your personal note.

You recall in the section on business card design, I said I like to make mine into a "mini-brochure." A big reason is that when the card arrives in the thank-you note it helps not only give contact info for me so they know who to appreciate for the thank-you note. They are also re-educated on what I do so I'll be top-of-mind when they need me. I strongly contend this is of benefit to you too.

What should I write ...?

You may be asking at this point, what exactly am I "thanking" someone I just met for doing? Just for the opportunity to meet them! We want to acknowledge them for the time they spent with us, and just remind them how much we respect their time and value their acquaintance. Your goal should be to sound as personal and sincere as possible, so the more specific you can be the better. If you want to work in a compliment to the person or something that can help them, like a web address that relates to your conversation, you'll distinguish yourself even further.

Great to meet you at Rotary the other day! I really enjoyed hearing about that new product you folks are launching. I had a chance to visit your website and was even more impressed! I've enclosed a newspaper clipping I saw when I was on the West Coast a while back that I thought you might find interesting because it's similar to what we talked about!

Thanks for taking time to chat for a few minutes at the networking event! I was impressed at how many people knew you and appreciate your taking time to introduce me to some of your acquaintances. Good luck and I'll look forward to seeing you at the next meeting.

Just wanted to let you know how much I enjoyed spending a little time with you at the networking event Thursday. I thought the speaker was very good and was equally impressed in visiting with you afterwards how much of what she advocated you already do! I predict your success will continue and please don't hesitate to let me know if I can be of any help.

I sure enjoyed visiting with you at the Chamber of Commerce event the other evening and hearing about what you do! I hope our paths cross again soon! I also look forward to us helping one another in the future if the opportunity presents itself.

You get the idea. What you say is far less important than the fact that you took time to write it, so just make your goal to correspond via personal, hand written note as often as possible!

Reciprocation Vs. Compensation

What we hope happens, as we build our network, is that we receive all kinds of leads and, ultimately, business from those in our network. We also hope we can do the same for those in our network, and this is where the great game of networking becomes incredibly exciting and rewarding. Remember, you want your brand to stand for "problem-solver." You hope, of course, to reach your goals, and you'll find it's so much easier to do that when you help others reach their goals. You want to play a key role in helping others accomplish what they're after. That will help build your brand incredibly.

A question we end up having to address is how do we go about compensating one another for helping reach our goals? As you can imagine, this is a bit tricky. If you sell computer network systems and I sell pet rocks, the size of the sale may be very disproportionate. Say I send you a lead that turns into a multi-million dollar deal, I may expect you to send me a nice tribute of several thousand dollars. For that matter, sending me a commission, or referral fee, of several thousand dollars may just be how you do business, but it may cause me to feel a little obligated. Or inadequate. Or anything but equitable in our relationship. What happens when you then send me a nice piece of business, but it's nowhere near a multi-million dollar deal and the compensation I send you doesn't even come close? We may both end up with hard feelings or discomfort.

My advice is to avoid trying to compensate members of your network financially unless you have discussed a formal, specific strategic alliance. Trying to compensate equitably can cause problems like the situation just described. The best way to compensate is to reciprocate. Be sure to sincerely and profusely say "thank you," by at least a personal note, a phone call, maybe even by dropping by in person or taking the referrer to lunch. But I would suggest avoiding monetarily compensating members of your network. We build our networks to build our businesses, so the best thing to do is help one another get more business and leave it at that.

> *You can have anything in life you want if you will just help enough other people get what they want*—Zig Ziglar

Say "Thanks" Even If You Don't Get the Business

There's no greater compliment than to get a phone call from a prospect who names someone in your network and says they recommended you. This is a great honor, and should be appreciated as such. It would be an insult to your professional intelligence to say you know you *have* to give any business you get through a personal referral your very best effort, so I won't.

Very obviously, we need to be sure to say "thanks" to those members of our network who send us leads that turn into business. You will probably want to personally thank the person giving you the referral via phone call, and/or we might send them a note, or series of notes, that read something like,

> *Fred,*

> *Thank you very much for recommending me to Joan over at XYZ Industries. We have a meeting Thursday and I am anxious to discuss with her how I may be able to help. I am both grateful for the confidence you have placed in me and ever mindful that I am representing you as well as my own firm when I meet with any potential customer*

you send my way, and that will guide every action I take. I'll be sure to let you know how it goes!

This simple little note accomplishes several things. It shows you are a serious, professional player in the great game of networking, who actively seeks and actively appreciates referrals. It also shows you are safeguarding the best interests of the person who referred you, and will reassure them they made the right decision in referring you.

Once you've met with the person, you will again want to send some follow up correspondence. As you've probably guessed, you send a thank-you note to the prospect, whether you get the business or not. Just because there wasn't a fit between you and the prospect today doesn't mean there aren't plenty of people in their network to whom they can refer you, so remember you may not always make the sale, but you can always build your brand. It's also a good idea to get these follow-up notes in the mail the day after your appointment or by the week's end at the latest.

If you closed the business (and opened the relationship!) during your meeting, your note will obviously be a thank-you to your new customer for the business. That note might read something like what you see below, or you can say whatever makes you feel most comfortable. Something I'd advise you to NEVER say is "You won't regret this …" because that not only sounds trite, but that they might someday regret it probably wouldn't have crossed their minds until you said that!

Joan,

Thank you very much for the opportunity to do business with you. We are delighted to have added you to our customer family and look forward to helping you get all the benefits from [YOUR PRODUCT] we discussed in our meeting. I'll also be sure to drop Fred a line and thank him for making this relationship possible. I've enclosed another business card in case you need anything else from me, and I may drop you a line from time to time just to make sure things are going smoothly. Thanks again!

Even if you don't get the business, you can still build your brand. That's a very important thing many non-professional networkers fail to realize. I've heard of some who don't play our beloved game of networking at a professional level treating the prospect who isn't converted into a customer like the enemy. Frustration is natural. Nobody likes to "lose," but getting angry won't do any good, and bad-mouthing a prospect, who is undoubtedly a member of several other networks, will *never* result in a win in the long run. This is obviously not how you want to build your brand! You want those folks saying good things about you even if they don't become customers, because you know that they know and may recommend you to someone who can.

Here's how a note to a prospect who, unfortunately, didn't become our customer might read.

Joan,

Thank you very much for the opportunity to meet with you and get to know you and your organization better over the past few meetings. I wish there was a fit for us right now, but I appreciate your time and respect your decision. We'll be here for you any time if something changes, and you're welcome to contact me at your convenience if I can help you in any way. I wish you continued success!

We could mention that we'll look forward to seeing them in the business community at other networking events. This subtly tells them that we have no hard feelings over not getting the business, and that they need not avoid us at future events! We can also make a point of sending them articles, or other things from time to time, just to stay familiar. A relationship not coming together today doesn't mean it won't someday! Be positive.

Similarly, we need to make sure we let the member of our network who referred us know how things went like we promised in a previous note. And just as we need to send a note to a prospect, whether they become a customer or not, we also need to keep the referrer in the loop. Here's an example of a note we might send to a referrer who sent us a prospect we converted into a customer:

> *Fred,*
>
> *Thanks a million for introducing me to Joan. We met last week and I'm excited to report that we helped find the solution she was looking for. The confidence she has in you was undoubtedly a big help in making that happen, and I am very grateful for the trust you placed in me to make the recommendation. Thank you again for being such a big help.*

Notice we don't say we "sold" Joan. Nobody likes to be "sold," but they don't mind *investing* in a *solution*. You may prefer other wording, but I would avoid using words like "sold." We have done more with this simple note than simply thanking Fred, though that is the main reason we sent it. Fred deserves our heartfelt thanks, and by sending him the note, we have also reaffirmed that his recommendation of us was the right decision. He knows we're the kind of professional who will appreciate anything we send him. Everyone loves to play for a winning team. Now Fred gets to stand in the winner's circle with us! It is also possible, if not downright *probable*, that Fred will call us up and say, "Hey, way to go! Here are some more folks you need to go see ...", and supply us with more and more leads.

But what if we don't get the business? What if, despite our best efforts and Fred's endorsement, things just don't pan out and the sale isn't made? Do we call Fred up and chew him out for wasting our time on a deadbeat like Joan? No, no, no. We are still very grateful for Fred's taking time to refer us and that's what we want to focus on. Fred probably thinks highly of, or at least knows, Joan very well, otherwise he would not have referred us. The last thing we ever want to do is say anything negative about a member of someone else's network. We will much more rapidly reach our goals if we invest our energy in celebrating all the good things that happen to us rather than stewing and hissing about the bad. Here's an example of what we might say in a personal note to a member of our network who referred us to a prospect we didn't convert into a customer:

Fred,

Thank you again for helping me connect with Joan. We met last week and had some very good discussion, but it doesn't look like we are going to be able to get her organization involved in one of our solutions right now. It was very nice to meet her and I greatly appreciate the confidence you placed in me to have recommended me to her. Thank you for your trust and I'll look forward to seeing you soon.

Fred will appreciate your letting him know how things turned out. Because you've been so good about appreciating him all along the way, he may even feel a little obligated to go find you some more leads that you will be able to close! Or, he may give you some valuable insight into what might have been done differently to get the business. Whatever the outcome, the important thing is to acknowledge and appreciate those who help you along the way.

A Note About Notes ...

As you read some of the sample personal/thank-you notes I've shared in this book, you may find yourself saying, "That's a little too generic to suit me," Or, "I'd never say it like that." If we were in the same room and you said that, I'd say that's music to my ears! Good for you! That's precisely what you should be thinking as you read anything in this book or any other how-to book! You should consider the ideas presented, but run them through your own "filters" and keep only what you're comfortable with, or what works for you. It can't be "the" system, "a" system, or "Dr. Burt's" system; it has to be "YOUR" system!

CAUTION ...

As firm a believer as I am in the power of networking, and as passionately as I love to play it, I do have to say that though I readily add members to my network, I'm kind of a tough sell when it comes to getting me to send them business. That's something I encourage you to consider too. I make a point of trying to patronize trusted members of my network whenever possible, but I have to say they really have to prove themselves before I'll roll the dice with my own reputation by referring them to other members of my network. If you're adding *professionals* to your network, they will respect and understand this and won't put undue pressure on you for referrals. Just as they know, if they refer you to others, both reputations are on the line in doing so, and too much is at stake. Look forward to the joy of referring business to others, but do so cautiously.

Databases—Your Most Valuable Asset!

Collecting business cards at an event is a great start, and using them to send personal notes to the people you meet is a must when it comes to investing your time. Another big must is that you don't just let those business cards you collect pile up and go to waste! You've got to maximize their use by putting them in a database that can be mined for optimal value.

If you look up the definition of a database in a marketing textbook, it is usually defined as "a collection of organized, readily accessible information," or something like that. Notice that nowhere in that definition does it say a database has to be computerized, digital, or mechanical, in any way. A shoe box filled with business cards stapled to index cards, organized alphabetically is an organized, readily accessible collection of information. And such a system is certainly better than nothing. However, there are far too many advantages to having your database in a software program to not consider that medium.

Database programs today are inexpensive in terms of their investment and are virtually invaluable in their potential payoff to your career and your business. They are truly an asset! They let you keep track of and effectively manage so many valuable relationships.

I'm often asked what database programs I like best and I used to readily answer with the product I'd used for over 10 years. After some disappointments with that product, however, I have since changed to what I think is a superior product, and I am not too sure there aren't even better solutions out there, I just haven't had time to research. You're welcome to e-mail me at the time you're reading this and you'll get my latest opinion on what database program is my pick. Or you can take this advice which I think is a much better use of your time: Do your own homework! Take a look at as many systems as possible, test-drive as many as possible. Ask as many people who use products you're considering what they like about it. Also ask them if they could change one thing about it, what would it be? Ask about backup, storage, security, and transferability. Ask about how well the program integrates with other things you'll want to do, like mail merges and the printing of labels. Essentially, as Dr. Stephen Covey advocates, "Begin with the end in mind." Think about your desired end result, then work backwards to build the system that will help you do that.

If that breathless paragraph sounds like database selection is too daunting a task, or if you're a newcomer to the great game of networking, here's my advice: Pick a simple program like a spreadsheet and start building your system from there. Make sure you can save your data in a transferable format like, comma separated value (csv), so you can move that info to another program if you find one you like better later on. Then you're set to get started.

Your database should minimally include the following:

Contact's name

Company or Organization

Title

Address

All means of telephone contact

Website

e-mail

A field for text notes (very important!)

These basic points let you capture the relevant information about people you meet. At the very least, this lets you know how to contact them when you need to, and makes it easy to sort by company name or person's name. You'll find that as your number of contacts grows (and grows rapidly!), it's hard to remember who everyone is, who does what, and all that. Having answers to these kinds of questions in an electronic database makes it easier and faster to search for things. I strongly recommend having some form of personal data system (PDA) that you can carry with you at all times, because you are playing the great game of networking at all times. Because the PDA was designed for this kind of access, the instructions that come with the device will have plenty of suggestions on how to best utilize your information.

A database with a text field that allows for keyword searches is really important, just because it's easier to do searches this way. For example, you may someday have a need, or be contacted by a member of your network who has a need, for a particular service. Let's say, for example, it's a need for a CPA. You can type the words "CPA," or "Accountant," and the PDA will search all the fields for accountant. This includes not only the CPAs and Accountants you have in your database, but if you've put some remarks in a text field, it'll pick those up too. For example, imagine you've had a conversation with a person in your network who is not an accountant, but told you "If you ever need a good CPA, let me know because I've got one I'd sure recommend." You could have noted that in your notes field of your database ("Murray has a CPA he recommends"). Some time later you or someone else may be looking for a CPA. You may remember that Murray had a good suggestion. Or, you may just remember that you visited with someone about a CPA, but you might not remember much else. You can simply type in "CPA" and your search would locate the term "CPA" anywhere it appears in your database. I most often use the notes field to jot down where and when I met this person. Capture anything that helps you distinguish a contact into your notes/text fields and you have one more easy way to find them when searching.

As you put your database to use, you'll determine how to best customize its structure and content to meet your needs, so be prepared for flexibility. This is also why your initial choice of database really isn't that important. What is important is that transferring its contents in a comma separated value (csv) or other transferable format is possible.

It's pretty obvious that your database is a great asset, especially when put to work. The sad thing is, many of us take for granted, or undervalue, the asset our database represents. In reality, we should take the number of names in our database and multiply them by at least $8 each. If we had to go out and buy that list or build it from scratch, acquiring each name would easily cost us $8 and probably a lot more, perhaps as high as $35 *per name*! Maybe more! When you consider the time it took you to personally acquire many of the names on your list. Put a pencil to your list using any figure you like and you'll see you have some real value there. Bottom line: Your database is an asset that is to be guarded and maximized!

Advanced Fields

Fields you may want to add later on include: Industry, names of network members' spouses, children, schools attended, education level attained, hometown, civic groups and charities with which they're involved, hobbies, etc. You can always add these later. In fact, finding these things out gives you some great topics for future conversations. Your specific industry, business, or situation may also lead you to develop fields customized to meet your needs, so you may want to let that guide your database development. I'm no expert in this, but I have had different degrees of success and have learned some lessons the hard way when it comes to databases, so you're welcome to e-mail me with any questions, and I'll see what I can offer, or I'll put you in touch with one of my colleagues who can help you.

Do a Quarter Each Quarter

Here's a little method shared with me by sales guru Bob Oros (www.moregrossprofit.com) to help you stay in touch with your entire database. Send out a postcard once in a while so you keep your database updated. Information isn't power. Only actionable information is power, and if the information is out of date or otherwise inaccurate, its use to you is diminished.

Here's a tip on how to contact your entire database: Do a quarter each quarter. Break your mailing list into "quarters" based on the alphabet (A-G, H-M, N-S, T-Z), then do a quarter each quarter. Each quarter, do a mailing of some kind to one quarter of the members of your database. For example, mail to A-G in the January, H-M in April, N-S in July, T-Z in October, or whatever suits your needs. By year end you will have contacted your entire data base at least once that year. You should always use the Postal Service's RETURN SERVICE REQUESTED feature. That way, if recipients have changed addresses, you will receive the mail piece back with a label from the Postal Service attached showing the recipient's new address. There are other services that will actually forward your mail piece and then send you a separate postcard with the updated mail information, and these are great too if you don't mind paying for them, but RETURN SERVICE REQUESTED is a very dependable and *free* feature that helps maximize the power of your database!

Other Communication

It should be obvious after reading this section that our goal in developing and utilizing a database is to have personal and consistent communication with those in our network. Below are some ways for you to stay in front of the members of your network while subtly reminding them of the value you bring to them.

Look for news

Any time you see something that could be of interest to a member of your network, get it in their hands! Even if the article content seems too obvious to be of value, send it to them anyway! Your network member may have been on vacation for a week and missed an article or something that could really have helped them, and you can come to their rescue. Or they may be so busy, they just don't have time to stay on top of as many publications as they'd like, which is highly possible. If they have already seen it, they will still appreciate your thinking of them.

And when they ARE the news ...

One great way to be a hero to the contacts in your database and those you want to add to your network is to recognize them when they make the news. When you see any kind of favorable or interesting press regarding someone you either are already acquainted with or would like to be, let them know you noticed!

Clip the article and send it to them in a personal note in which you congratulate them. This is a good way to recognize the person and get your name in front of them. This idea is time-honored and earned for itself a place in the networking ideas hall of fame years ago, so we know it works and is respected. The only problem I have with it is that chances are, other people know about this hall-of-fame technique, will see the article and will send it to the person too. This is not all bad. Your gesture will still be appreciated, but here's an idea I've found to be far more effective.

First, cut out the article and, if possible, get the front page of the newspaper, or cover of the magazine, or whatever is the main page. Paste the article under the heading as neatly as possible so that even if the article wasn't front-page news before, it looks like it now! Or, if it's a magazine, paste the cover next to the article. You may want to practice using a hobby knife, and doing this on articles you don't intend to send. This way, you can get really good at doing it. Or you may want to take it to the local copy shop and have them do it for you. I typically choose this option because it only costs a few dollars.

Then, have this magnificent, newly created piece of journalism laminated! Because newspapers today are designed to be biodegradable, they tend to biodegrade pretty doggone fast. A week from now, the clipping may be yellowed, brittle, and not something the recipient is in love with any more. Plus, the ink tends to get on the recipient's fingers and that is not the association we want for our brand. Instead, we want them to open our big envelope with this nicely laminated tribute to their accomplishment and be wowed! And, to make sure they remember who "wowed" them, you need to be sure to laminate your business card on the back of the article. That way, every time they pick it up to admire it, they'll see your card on the back and remember your thoughtfulness! You can even write a little note of congratulations on the backside under the laminate, if you desire.

Do you seriously think they would dare part with a fine piece of recognition like this? Absolutely not! They'll find a place for it in the office! In fact, your sending it actually gives them a reason to prominently display it! Someone comes in and asks about it, or remarks about it, which is exactly why they wanted it displayed in the first place, you give them an "out." They can give the person who asked about it an "aw shucks" shrug and say, "Oh yeah, that. It's an article about me … I wouldn't have it up but this nice person sent it to me and it seemed kind of rude not to do something with it …" and they'll probably show them your card on the back just to prove their modesty. Then they can spend time oh so humbly telling the person who asked all about it! And you made that possible!

Get this—You may even find that the person who asked about the article, and how it is showcased, asks about you! You may get all kinds of mileage out of it and it will only cost you a few dollars.

6

Advanced Networking: Positioning Yourself as the Game!

Advanced Networking Strategies & Tactics

I've had people tell me they planned to purchase this book mainly for this section. This section tends to yield the most favorable e-mails and thank-you's from seminar attendees. This is especially true for those who have already established themselves in the great game of networking and are looking to take their games to the next level. As your networking coach in the great game of networking, hearing this pleases me greatly not only because it means you get a significant return on your investment in this book, but because it helps you maximize the potential of your personal brand. That allows you to not only have professional success, but to really enjoy life and business. Remember, we call it the great *game* of networking for a reason.

As you play the great game of networking, you may realize that there are others out there doing the same thing. You may have competitors who network in the same venues as you, who may even employ some of the same tactics you use, and who may be less than interested in forming any kind of strategic alliance with you. They may have even read some of the same excellent books or attended the same networking seminars you have. My bet, however, is that they lack the thing that makes you a success, and the key that will help you build on your accomplishments: the ability to APPLY what you learn by taking ACTION! This section shows you how to move into "graduate level" networking so you are constantly reinventing yourself, and ensuring the marketplace equates you with the category you represent.

I subtitled this section "Positioning yourself as the Game," because I want you not to just PLAY the game of networking, but to be equated WITH the great game of networking in your area! When people think of excellent networkers, my goal is for them to think first of you, and to use you as the standard against which all professional networking is compared.

Incidentally, the marketing word for that is, "positioning." Marketing legends Al Reis and Jack Trout deserve credit for first introducing the word in a strategic, business context, in their classic book, *The 22*

Immutable Laws of Marketing. Positioning is not what we do to a product, but is being equated with the category in the mind of the marketplace. For example, when companies think of "overnight delivery," they think of FedEx. FedEx owns the words "overnight" in the mind of the customer, though there are several competitors who offer overnight delivery at a comparable level. What you want to do is become equated with the category you represent. For example, if you are in the insurance industry, you want those in your network to think first of you when they have a need, think about insurance, or are asked for their opinions about insurance. The greater your visibility is, the stronger the association in the customers' minds.

Opportunities to increase your visibility are everywhere. In this section we'll examine the reasons why you should find an avenue to put your leadership skills to work. When I say "leadership," that doesn't mean you have to be the chairperson or president of the organization, or even chair a committee. But it does mean you should build your personal brand by demonstrating your talents and your dependability to further the mission of a cause or organization. We'll also discuss the pros and cons of "moving up" in organizations.

Actively being involved in leadership is something about which I am very passionate. Some of my fondest memories as a business owner are related to my playing the great game of networking at the leadership level. My work as a volunteer not only did great things for my business, but it let me spend quality time with influential people who I might not have even been able to meet otherwise. I won't take your time here to tell the whole story of my volunteer experience, but as my biography in the back of the book shows, I've had some great opportunities, and some great press, as a result. That's why I am so confidently recommending you take your networking game to the next level by becoming actively involved somewhere.

Increased visibility enables you to:

- Be viewed as a leader in the community and in your profession

- Co-brand yourself with the organization
- Grow professionally and personally

Be viewed as a leader ...

Just being an active volunteer gets you some excellent press! If the organization publishes a newsletter (online or printed versions), chances are somewhere in there is a list of the different activities, events, and the volunteers who make them happen. Having your name show up every month in the newsletter tells the marketplace you are the kind of person people can depend upon and in whose corner they want to be. Many political offices are won solely on name recognition. Many purchase decisions are influenced the same way. It looks great to be able to say in your promotional materials, or on a proposal, that you are an active leader in your profession and in your community, and the prospects' ability to see your involvement for themselves can reassure them. In a later section, we'll discuss how to choose which activities may best meet your needs. Hear me now, believe me later, this is a good move for your career.

Co-brand yourself with the organization

In the mind of the prospect, you and the association are one and the same! Your volunteer efforts can result in your being able to leverage your time invested by taking advantage of the promotional efforts of the organization you serve. If the prospect sees a lot of promotion for the organization, then sees that you are involved with the organization, they will put you both at the same level. This is especially true if you are involved locally with national organizations. Your press may be local but your affiliation is national.

Grow professionally and personally

One of the things that appealed to me about essentially working for "free," as a volunteer for the organizations with which I was involved, was the excellent professional growth opportunities they presented. As a small business, there was a lot of great training I had the chance to receive as a volunteer at the expense of the organizations. Part of what made the experience so beneficial was that it put me next to other professionals who were at various experience levels or stages of growing their businesses, so we all had a chance to grow together while serving a common cause. Even though we sometimes had to wonder if all the time and effort was worth it, or if maybe we weren't taking a little too much time away from our paying activities, at those year-end banquets, or at the completion of a big project or event where we could all stand arm-in-arm and say, "Look what we did!", it was always worth it. In fact, though many of us went on to have greater success and recognition in our businesses, we still look back happily at those times when our time and energy were all we had to give. I can't wait for you to have this experience. You'll find there are both personal and professional benefits awaiting your volunteer efforts. They help remind us that we are playing the great game of networking to have professional success as a means to a life filled with the rewards of fond memories of working with people like us to serve a worthy purpose. As you young people say, volunteering is really where it's at, man. It's totally groovy and I dig it so much.

Getting involved

When we first opened our discussion of the great game of networking, I shared how exciting it is that the rules of networking had changed over the last quarter of a century or so. A great power shift took place in that the opportunity to have a network of contacts was no longer the sole property of the affluent. Volunteer activities are the same way! I remember reading this in Tom Peter's *The Pursuit of Wow* in 1994. He mentioned how the rules of networking were changing, using the example of how a real estate agent from a small firm could just as easily chair a million dollar charity event as the chairman of the board of the local bank from a long line of family bankers. This was very exciting news, especially for me and some of my friends who were starting businesses without a lot of capital at the time. And it turned out to be entirely true!

Present yourself to the leaders of the organizations with which you want to get involved using the same techniques we discussed under the guiding principles for networking. Go in with an attitude of service, and I assure you they'll put you to work quickly. You should expect to have to pay your dues first, though. Remember, those who are currently in leadership probably had to work their way up, and they will resent someone who thinks they can just walk up and grab the glory without earning their "spot" first. Go in with an attitude of service, roll up your sleeves and eagerly go to work, and you will ultimately benefit! It really is often as simple as stepping forward and offering your time and energy in many cases. As the famous Nike commercials always said, "Just Do it!"

Where to Plug In

Obviously, you want to pick the positions that give you the most exposure, with the most economical application of effort. A good idea is to pick something that closely aligns with either your brand (specifically your product or category), or a cause that effectively compliments what you do, and helps you best leverage your time while granting you the most visibility.

Sometimes this is as easy as volunteering; However, you are going to be competing with others who are doing the same thing, so it may take a while to get the exact position you want. Some committees may give so much great visibility and benefit that there are more eager volunteers than there are spots to fill, so you may end up having to wait a little. It's ok to be assertive, but handle this with reserve. Don't try to elbow your way in because your brand is always at stake. Be patient and wait your turn, or find another place to plug in.

Great Salespersons Need Apply

New members are the life blood of any organization. Membership dues mean cash flow and funding for projects, and new members mean more contacts with whom current members can network. If you are an excellent salesperson, you will do an excellent job of growing the organization, and you will very quickly make a name for yourself. One of my networking buddies, who did sales training, took it upon himself to chair the membership committee. He not only turned in record-breaking new membership numbers personally, he used this leadership opportunity as a way to showcase his training techniques, providing the members of his committee with the valuable benefit of free sales training. In this case, my friend the sales trainer, his volunteers, and the organization all won, which is what the great game of networking is all about. I also remember vividly how impressed the veteran members of the organization were with this effort. My friend quickly moved into leadership, his sales continued to go up, AND he reaped the benefits of this legendary feat for as long as he was involved in the organization. For years, they recalled the dramatic impact he made on membership when he initially joined, and that became the brand story they told for him. There are probably similar opportunities for YOU to make a splash, and leverage your accomplishments, so look for them.

Service over selling?

If selling is not your thing, there are still plenty of opportunities for greater visibility. In fact, I have purposely avoided direct selling as a volunteer activity in most organizations in which I volunteer for a simple reason: If I'm going to sell for someone, it's going to be me! Seriously, I have seen some of my colleagues get into organizations and get so fired up about being recognized for selling more memberships, or selling something that raises money on behalf of the organization, and getting some silly plastic trophy or something, that they overlook their own business! My thought is, I want my brand to be viewed for service rather than selling. I tend to prefer, and I suggest you consider, committees and activities that involve "service" over "selling."

One such offering that you'll find in most organizations is an "ambassador" committee. Though they may not be called the "ambassador" committee, Chambers of Commerce typically have a volunteer group whose duties are to reach out to existing, or new members, and help them get involved with the organization, thus getting the most from their membership. This is a fantastic way to meet people in a non-threatening way, and to showcase your brand as that of a service-driven individual. Imagine how much I will appreciate you, a volunteer who isn't being paid anything, contacting me to help me get the most from my membership! I will be put at ease, because I may be a shy person who knows he needs to be involved, but just doesn't feel comfortable taking the initiative, or just doesn't know who to call. Thanks to you, I will now know at least *one* person at the next event I attend, and you being the highly trained professional player of the great game of networking you are, you will be my guide, mentor, and host at the next event I attend. Just imagine the kind of branding goodwill I will eagerly share on your behalf.

Of course, if the organization has no formal "ambassador" type group, there is NOTHING saying YOU can't make a serious effort to help others get the most from their membership in an organization! Do this and you'll grow your brand equity in the process! This relates to the "look for strangers and be an ambassador" principle discussed earlier. The potential payoff for taking this kind of initiative is truly limited only by the amount of elbow grease you want to put into it.

As your business grows, and your time becomes more limited, you will need to be very cautious to make sure you invest your time with the best prospects for your business. But, when you are new to a group or new to a market, you will benefit tremendously by getting as wide an exposure as you can to help generate grass-roots marketing messengers for you.

Take on the cruddy task ... And blast onto the scene!

One thing that can really help you distinguish yourself and your brand is to take on the job nobody else wants, or that most people avoid. There are less visible, less fun, more labor intensive projects that have to be done, and finding those to do them are often a challenge that an organization faces. The organization's challenge may very well be your opportunity!

I saw a vivid example of this early in my volunteer career, in an organization with which I was involved. One of the projects this organization did every year was an annual banquet. It was an event we volunteers looked forward to every year, and was a big-budget, signature event of the organization. It also was a whole lot of work, though, and a lot of volunteers (including your favorite networking author!) tended to shy away from it, because it was so time and labor intensive. Because it was so hard to get volunteers, as you can imagine, it was also extremely tough to get leaders who wanted to coordinate and chair the event.

Fortunately for the organization, my colleague wasn't afraid of a challenge and she stepped up to chair the event. She did a great job with it, and did wonders for her brand.

Were my colleague in the catering or event planning business, this would be a logical fit, wouldn't it? And had either of those been her profession, it would serve as a superb example of self-promotion. What better way to showcase one's abilities than to blast onto the scene, use one's own expertise to solve a problem, and then have a living testimonial of one's abilities? That is definitely something for you to think about. If there is some need the organization has that your product/service can fill, that's a great way to jump in and quickly make a name for yourself.

Noteworthy, however, is that my colleague was not in either the catering or event planning business, which makes the story even better! She was actually in real estate! Yep, a real estate agent took the bull by the horns and chaired a banquet committee. At first blush, you might look at that act and think it was imprudent for her to spend her time in a project so drastically unrelated to her field. What happened, though, is a great lesson for us all, and one I never forgot. For, you see, what my colleague showed us all was that she was a dependable, hard worker! She did this great job, and created a great deal of "buzz" from the attendees. People clamored to learn more about her and her business. The dramatic message this act carried to the marketplace was, "If she'll work that hard for free as a volunteer coordinating a banquet, think how hard she will work for me if she's my real estate agent!" A lot of drive in the short term resulted in long-term power branding for her, and that is the kind of thing that can make YOU an all-star in the great game of networking, too! So look for that task everyone else considers cruddy, and see how you can turn it into an opportunity.

If they'll work that hard for free, think how hard they'll work for me!—Burtism

Leadership

Type in "leadership" in the search engine of any online bookseller and you'll get several thousand titles. This is a very popular, if not over-done, subject, and the definition of leadership seems to vary also. To me, a leader is someone who offers their best in any position. You can do that as the head of an organization or in any other role, but the necessity again is ACTION. Leaders are everywhere, and leaders are needed everywhere.

I strongly urge you to be a leader in your field, whatever you do. Again, because you are the kind of professional who invests in a book like this, I believe I can say with a fair amount of certainty that you are the kind of person who is a great ambassador for your profession, and a LEADER in your profession. Because that is just one of the many strengths I'm betting you have, you should strongly consider taking an active leadership role in your community.

You can accomplish this by getting involved. As you attend these events and join organizations (after they have demonstrated value to you, of course), you should see that value exists in taking a more visible role as a volunteer. You may also want to set a goal for yourself of moving up in the organizations in which you serve, which is where we're going next!

> *A leader is someone who has earned the right to have follow-ers.*—Dwight D. Eisenhower

Moving Up the Ladder

Taking a hard look at what the organization has to offer after you take a hard, thoughtful look at exactly what you want to accomplish, is a good idea. I really hope you have a goal of moving into a position that gives you the opportunity to lead your fellow volunteers. This was a big help to my business, as a youngster making his way in the marketplace, not only because it helped me acquire business, but also because it helped me get some excellent developmental training I would not have had the time or money to get in any other way. If you're a small business owner, you might consider the side-benefit of serving as a volunteer leader. There is also nothing in the world like the feeling that comes from knowing you and a group of volunteers gave your time to accomplish something bigger than your own interests. Part of what makes it such unique leadership training, by the way, is that you are leading your peers! You can't really "fire" volunteers! Some of my fondest business memories involve my service in and leadership for volunteer organizations. I sincerely hope you get to experience this too, so think about moving up the "ladder" in organizations by assuming additional responsibility.

"You're a board member for a year ..."

Ultimately, I encourage you to become the chair, or president, or whatever the highest ranking position is within the organizations/associations in which you are involved. The reason is simple. You're a board member for a year, but you're a past-president for the rest of your life! If you notice some of the publications and recognition in the organizations in which you're networking, you'll see that past-chairs, past-presidents, and what have you, hold a special place of honor. Often the names of those who served on the boards of these organizations have faded from memory, but past-presidents are typically remembered from now on. I've been in organizations that dedicated a page of the website or newsletter to recognizing past-presidents, and some places even ask past-presidents to stand and be recognized at luncheons or banquets or serve as ex-officio board members. Serving as the president of a volunteer board can be a time-consuming challenge, but it can also be well-worth it in terms of the brand equity you will be able to leverage for years to come. If you've been to my workshops, you know this is something I am very passionate about, because I see so many great things in your future that can come from it. Again, you're a board member for a year, but you're a past-president for the rest of your life! I will probably write more on these "advanced networking" subjects in future books, once I hear what readers like you have to say about what I've written here and whether you found it helpful or not. But if you have specific questions I can answer now, feel free to send me an e-mail and I'll do what I can to offer some guidance.

A word of caution

On the other hand, recall that I said to think long and hard about what you want. If you end up giving more time to your service work than your business/career or family, you'll end up with a short-term gain, at best. I believe the pro's outweigh the con's by a long way, but I also want to help you make the right decisions. So. make sure you focus on what you really want. Don't serve just to get a title, or your name in the paper, or for one more line on your resume or bio. The organization won't get your very best, and you'll have only a lackluster experience. Your energy could be far better spent somewhere else if that is your motivation.

There is nothing at all wrong with expecting some personal payoff for your involvement. It has to be win-win, and I never discourage anyone from getting as much mileage from their involvement as possible. What I think you'll find, though, is an eventually diminishing return on the investment you make of your time and energy. For one thing, there is sort of a "rule of 3" when it comes to bios, resumes, credibility pieces, etc. The reader, or customer, is only going to be interested in, impressed by, or even remember only about 3 things per category. I think a goal of being "president," or "chair," or whatever of about 3 organizations, or 3 events, or committees, or whatever is really enough. If your pedigree is too full of volunteer items, they run together in the mind of your prospects. They may wonder how you can be good at your real job, and when you find time to do actual work! In fact, if you're too active, they may just assume you're an employee of the organization. Talk about a diminishing return!

Burnout isn't a game!

Another huge caution is burnout. That probably goes without saying, but folks like you and me who like to serve can sometimes have a hard time saying "no" to taking on a new task. Not just because we love to help, but because we hate to turn down a challenge. We may find this taking time away from our more profitable goals or, more importantly, from those in our lives who care about us. Burnout is no game! It is a serious circumstance with serious personal and professional consequences. If you are not at your best, you cannot help anyone. Be very mindful of how you use your time, so playing the great game of networking is as fun as it should be. Remember, we call it the great GAME of networking for a reason!

Sponsorship!

We're departing a bit from simply networking and veering more into marketing here, but I think this is worth discussing and will ultimately be valuable to you. Many times, as you become more involved with organizations, you are either approached about, or on your own become interested in, sponsoring an event. This can be a good way to maximize your exposure and leverage the brand equity you have built through your networking. It also endears you to the organization offering the sponsorship.

Picking and choosing

Just as you choose your networking arenas carefully, and based on the ability of the attendees to contribute to your goals, sponsorship demands thoughtful consideration. This is true because while your networking is often free, or close to it, sponsorship requires a specific and potentially significant monetary investment, so deliberation is definitely in order. This is something I've done with some success, but I also have to confess that I've wasted a lot of money on sponsorships, largely because I didn't put enough thought into them or implement them in a way that made the most of my investment. I'd like to help you avoid my mistakes!

A good idea is to know as much as you can about who will be at the event, or will have exposure to the media you use, as your sponsorship in advance. You should also consider how the sponsorship could pay for itself. If this additional exposure can help solidify your brand, then it is a good investment. You can tout for some time that you are a supporter of the organization who is willing to go the extra mile, and offer additional support in the form of a sponsorship. You can mention that you were a sponsor of that golf tournament for a whole year, or maybe even two years on your website, or through other promotional vehicles. The lesson is obviously any time you do a sponsorship, make sure you have a plan to get as much long-term exposure as you can and you see some ultimate payoff.

Sponsoring an event of attendees who are not prospects for you, of attendees who may not be valuable additions to your network, or who already know you and what you do may be a poor use of your sponsorship dollars. That is a business fact and you need to be ever mindful.

What's just as big a waste of money as sponsoring an event of non-prospects, though, is to be involved with the right event aimed at the right prospects, but be just one of a whole bunch of sponsors, and end up lost in the shuffle. One of the first sponsorships I bought shortly after founding my company was at one of the big local golf tournaments. I spent around 300 bucks, which I thought was a bargain, considering the exposure I would get and the crowd that would attend. I'll never forget how excited I was to see my "name in lights." I walked in and there I was, waaaaaay down on the banner with about 75 or 80 other $300 sponsors!

I won't bore you with the other dumb, ego-driven, and thus wasteful, sponsorship expenditures I've made, but I have learned my lesson and I hope you learn it without spending thousands of dollars before you do.

Trade-outs!

Sometimes you can work a trade for a sponsorship. As a market researcher, organizations were often eager to let me do an event survey, or membership survey, in exchange for something like mention in the program or newsletter, or even annual dues. You may be in a business that lends itself well to a trade-out for a membership or sponsorship, and if so, this is a great way to get valuable exposure with no cash outlay. Some organizations are eager to do this, some refuse to do this, but asking won't cost you anything. When you do ask, do your best to showcase your proposal in a way that shows how the value the organization, and its members, far outweighs the amount of the sponsorship you are asking for trade.

Guerilla Sponsorships

If I lost all my credibility earlier when I confessed that I had blown thousands of dollars on big sponsorships that yielded little or even nothing, let me redeem myself here with some very cost-effective, high-payoff ideas that have worked for me and may work for you, too!

One thing I love to do, though I must disclose I didn't come up with this idea myself, is to send a reminder postcard to people about upcoming events. Where is it written that only the organization is allowed to notify attendees of the event? Nowhere! And no organization is going to be offended that you are working at your own expense to increase their attendance. This is a simple, powerful, and often over-looked way to keep your name in front of your mailing list while doing a favor to the people who are on it. This idea has actually grown in importance and appreciation from the recipients, because many organizations have moved away from any non-electronic communication because it has become too costly. This may be the exact reason why you want to develop your own mail piece about an event. With all the SPAM filters on e-mail systems these days, your notification may be the only way they hear about the event. Don't be surprised if they tell you, "I wouldn't have known about the meeting if it wasn't for you", as they thank you.

Here's how to make it work: Say you're a member of a group who has a monthly luncheon. For that matter, who says you have to be a member? Develop a simple postcard that reminds attendees of the date, and send it to them, either well ahead of the event and the communication the organization hosting the event would send, or send it right before the event as a last-minute reminder. The key is to distinguish your communication from that of the host of the event. I like the post-card approach. It's very cost effective, and it's brief, which usually means it gets read! You may want to experiment with the size of the postcards, too, and let your goals be your guide. For example, you can very cost-effectively do 3x5 size postcards (4 per 8 ½ x 11 page) or you can do an oversized card like a 6.5 x 11 in order to stand out from the recipient's other mail. What size you do is up to you, but try to do something to make it stand out.

As far as the copy, a simple reminder or invitation is really all you want to do. You may be tempted to cram the piece full of promotional messages in an effort to get the most from your investment. Fight that temptation. If it looks too much like a promotional piece, it could diminish the effect you're shooting for. Instead, make the postcard all about them with your logo and web address as the signature on the card. Doing something that encourages them to visit your website and learn more about you is a good idea, and you can do that without a lot of copy. For that matter, you could even have a downloadable map on how to find the event. Do it however you like, but I really think you'll find a clean, concise piece that makes the recipient the star will serve you best. Remember, your goal is to help others so they will want to do the same for you.

Unofficial Co-Sponsorship

There may also be a way for you to obtain a degree of "co-sponsorship" with an organization without being an official sponsor. Be careful and be very professional in how you approach this, but you may find there are some great and very inexpensive ways to get your name in front of the group without having to invest significantly or even officially.

For example, you might donate pens, notepads, or anything that helps the attendees get the most from the event. A professional attendee like you would never do this, but it's surprising how many folks attend a meeting and don't bring a pad or pen. You might be able to solve one or both of their problems, and wind up co-branded with the event as a result. Just imagine at each place, at each table, a pad, pen, or both with your logo on it as an aid to the attendees which just happen to serve as a subtle reminder of who you are and what you do. Or you could just donate your pens to the registration table or be sure to put them in the hands of as many attendees that need them. Your promotional products representative can help you with ideas like this. I have a great firm I use, and I'd be happy to pass along their information if you need it.

A caution, however, is to be sure you get the permission of the organization before you attempt anything like this! If you just start putting out your materials without authorization, you may find yourself in an embarrassing situation. Many organizations have rules about this, and many require a paid sponsorship to do such things because they recognize the significant opportunity it presents. Smaller organizations may not have that big a problem with it, but still, get permission! Not doing so could position you in the minds of the attendees and the organization as an opportunist, a rude self-promoter, or worse, and that is NOT where you want to be. So just ask. The worst thing that can happen is they say "No." Frankly, you'll probably find your personal networking is by far the most effective promotional tool you use, but I have also observed and had personal experience with how some unofficial co-sponsorship and tactics can compliment your networking activities and can essentially co-brand you with the organizations to which you belong.

Speaking of co-branding, here's a free thing you can do that will help set you apart: Always meet the speaker! And do so well *before* he or she gets to the platform. The more homework you do the better the relationship you can build with the speaker at the event, but even if you don't know much about the speaker, simply thanking them for being there and letting them know you're looking forward to hearing their talk can be a great way to not only build rapport, but to do some co-branding. Impress the speaker as a seasoned professional player of the great game of networking and he or she may mention you from the podium. I have used this strategy a lot and it really does wonders for your visibility and credibility. Even if the speaker stinks, he or she will be gone at the end of the event and you can stick around as the local expert.

I have some other ideas, and would be happy to offer you some personal suggestions if you want to e-mail me, but since this is a networking book and not a guerilla marketing book, I won't go into a lot of detail here. Little nuggets like this are exactly what I will be covering in my BLOG and e-newsletter, so you may want to subscribe to those.

Get some press!

Your networking, and especially your volunteerism, can get you some excellent visibility, and to fully capitalize on your efforts you should use that visibility to get publicity wherever you can! Chambers of Commerce and other organizations usually have newsletters that feature what the members are doing, specifically any volunteer driven activities. Typically, those volunteers who participate in an event get their pictures in the newsletter, so be sure you take advantage of as many of these as you can! If your activities are not being prominently featured in the publications of the organizations in which you're involved, make sure those who put the publications together know about you. Send your own photos and even your own write-ups to them. Don't be surprised if they re-write a lot of what you send, and don't get your feelings hurt if they don't feature what you do, but chances are they will appreciate your efforts, and your "ink" will come eventually.

If not, consider doing your own publication and feature yourself and your fellow volunteers! The more you feature your fellow volunteers, the more hands in which they'll help you put your self-sponsored newsletters.

If you are from a smaller town or live in a suburb, these newspapers love to feature locals who are making a difference in their professions and communities. Make friends, and stay friends, with anyone who does any kind of publication because getting featured gives you great credibility. You're reaching not only the reader, but any one of the approximately 250 or so people each reader knows! You'll be surprised at how far-reaching any press you get will be, and you'll be amazed at how people remember it long after it has run! You'll have people come up to you months and *months* afterward and say they "saw you in the paper the other day." Powerful stuff, and it's free!

It may even be worthwhile to see about hiring a public relations firm to help you grow and manage your exposure. Most will work on a per-hour basis. My experience has been that the cost is about what you'd pay a computer technician per hour, and you'll get a lot greater return on the investment you make in a public relations (PR) firm. You might even find a PR student who would take you on as a client so they'll have something for their portfolio. PR is a very powerful tool and you should incorporate PR into your marketing and networking.

> *Marketing is what you pay for, PR is what you pray for!*—Al Reis and Jack Trout, *The 22 Immutable Laws of Marketing*

Get Creative

As you're growing and succeeding, you'll find a lot of creative ways to get exposure, and maximize your networking efforts on your own. If nothing comes to mind right now, or if you're just getting started in the great game of networking, some of these advanced networking topics may not be as useful as they will in the future. To help spur your creativity, keeping a marketing journal like I mentioned earlier in the book is a great place to store the great ideas you see today from which you may profit tomorrow.

7

The Role of the Internet
In Networking

Going Digital

One of the most exciting developments in the Great Game of Networking is the inclusion of the world wide web, and other digital media, in our networking efforts. Like the internet itself, the exact usefulness of various media such as discussion groups, BLOGS, and online networks like Facebook and Myspace is evolving. Online networks appear to have provided greater utility for personal users rather than business users, so to say "time will tell" is probably the best bet at the time of this writing.

What has been a growing and valuable tool are the online discussion groups and "special interest groups" offered by some organizations. The National Speakers Association, for example, has several forums under their Professional Experts Group which lets those with specific interests communicate on those topics. For example, there is a group for speakers who also write. Members can chat online or post a question to which other members can respond, and do so from around the world. Many strategic alliances have been successfully formed through this means, and a lot of valuable information shared, because typically those who are communicating with one another are from markets with considerable distance from one another and are, as such, not direct competitors. As the world gets smaller thanks to technology, this trend will likely continue. Of course, because the world is getting smaller thanks to technology, and it is possible to compete in just about any market from our current location, less information may be exchanged in these kinds of forums as users become more guarded of their information, but I really doubt this will be the case.

Again, media like this is still evolving and finding its way, and though it will never completely replace face-to-face networking, and exactly how much credibility exists and how much trust can ultimately be placed in online networking, I do believe these media will be a valuable component of your networking efforts at some point in the future. I encourage you to do some research on your own and see what best matches your situation and your goals.

8
Conclusion

So when's the payoff?

You may be really excited to get busy putting to work the things we've talked about in this book. You may have started applying what you learned as you read it, and that's great too. A question you may have is, "Well, when will all this activity pay off?" A fair question, indeed, but exactly when your "payoff" will come is a little tough to predict. At the very least, you should feel confident and empowered by having some new techniques to put to work. You may indeed see results right away, or it may take a while. It may take longer than you had hoped, and you may in the longer term be pleasantly surprised with the huge returns on your networking investment that exceed your wildest expectations. The key is to keep working and diligently applying what you have learned here and what you learned on your own.

When you drop a pebble into a body of water, you'll notice the ripple effect goes all the way out to the ends of the body of water, then makes its way back to the center. It may not be visible to the naked eye, but the laws of physics tell us it happens. The larger the body of water, the more difficult it is to see, and the longer it takes the ripple to return to its point of origin, but eventually it does. Its energy takes it back to its point of origin. That's how your networking efforts will be. You'll put forth effort, your energy will expand, then it will eventually find its way back to you. A little patience will serve you well and will keep you looking and feeling like the professional you are. Make a ripple, and it will return to the source someday!

One thing you don't want to do is complain. Don't be that person, when asked how your business is going, or how your involvement in an organization is going, who grumbles and complains. Even if things aren't going so well, do NOT complain! Remember, there are no failures, only outcomes, and complaining will NOT help your brand.

Think about it. Nobody wants to play for a losing team! People want to do business with and refer winners. Always be upbeat and positive. Be thankful just for the chance to be in business, and that you have what it takes to play the great game of networking. Be patient, and the rewards will follow. How you act is what you'll attract!

I remember once, one of the members of my business network had gotten a bit down. She didn't feel like her involvement in the organization we were in together was producing any benefits, and she had become rather vocal about it to just about anyone who would listen, including some very public venues, for example, when we went around the room to introduce ourselves. *Yikes!* I pulled her aside and shared what I told you in the previous paragraph: Nobody wants to hire the company who needs the business! I encouraged her to publicly and enthusiastically *thank* them for any business they had sent her way. If she hadn't actually obtained business from her involvement, I told her to thank everyone for leads she had received, or to just say how excited she was to be a part of this organization. She began to do that and, all of a sudden, more business came her way. In fact, people loved playing for a winning team so much, people were bragging on my colleague and claiming they had sent her business even when they hadn't! This caused her brand to grow even more! People love to play for a winning team, so act like a winner and you'll be one!

Until we meet again ...

Recall when we started this journey, I said this was a book I am confident will help you, but it isn't the only answer out there! I appreciate your agreeing to take this journey with me, and I am excited to consider how the time and investment you have made can quickly pay off for you! But don't let your learning end there! I urge you to remember we are on a journey. Success is a journey, not a destination. Keep reading, keep studying, and keep growing! That way, you won't have to worry about the future. You can create your own future! If you look, you'll discover many, many good books that can help you on your journey, and not just business books. I've got several, listed on my website, that have helped me, and a lot of them were recommended to me by either someone I knew and respected, or were recommended in another book that was helpful. Helping you grow as a networker is the goal of this book, but if I can help you grow as a lifelong learner, that will make both of us and everyone whose lives we touch even bigger winners! By all means, feel free to drop me an e-mail now and then and let me know how it's going.

I also hope our paths cross in some arena someday, where you're playing the great game of networking. I'll look forward to meeting you, and I'll look forward to learning from YOU! In the meantime, thank you for allowing me to play a role in your professional development and I wish you all the success you can stand!

Your destiny awaits. *Go get 'em!*

Recommended Reading

7 Habits of Highly Effective People by Dr. Stephen Covey

7 Marketing Mistakes Every Business Makes and How to Fix Them by Terri Langhans

22 Immutable Laws of Marketing by Al Reis & Jack Trout

Bullseye! by Thomas Winninger

The Brainstorming Book by John Storm

Dig Your Well Before You're Thirsty by Harvey Mackay

Emily Post's The Etiquette Advantage in Business by Peggy Post & Peter Post

How to Drive Your Competition Crazy by Guy Kawasaki

How to Win Friends & Influence People by Dale Carnegie

Life is a Bowl of Choices by Kyle Eastham

Positioning by Al Reis & Jack Trout

The Psychology of Winning by Denis Waitley

The Pursuit of Wow by Tom Peters

Re-Imagine by Tom Peters

War of Art by Steven Pressfield

About the Author

Dr. Burt Smith, CME, CQM, PCM, (known affectionately as "Dr. Burt," to friends like you!) has owned Executive Marketing Information (EMI Research Solutions, LLC) since 1994. EMI is a market research and consulting firm, specializing in helping decision-makers increase profits through the measurement and improvement of customer satisfaction. He built the business almost entirely through networking, and is today one of the most recognized professionals in the Oklahoma Business Community.

He has served as a leader in several high-profile business organizations, including the Oklahoma City Chamber of Commerce, the American Marketing Association, and the Sales and Marketing Executives International. As president of the Oklahoma City Chapter of the American Marketing Association he led the chapter to its first national Chapter Excellence Award. He has represented Oklahoma six times at the AMA's International Leadership Summit. He received a commendation for his work on Governor Frank Keating's Small Business Commission.

In 2007, the Journal Record newspaper recognized Dr. Burt as part of its Centennial Class of 39 "Achievers Under 40," based on individual achievement, leadership, service and other contributions to the state of Oklahoma. He also appeared on the Metro Journal's "40 Under 40" list in 1997 and on the "40 Under 40" list for Oklahoma City Business in 2002.

Dr. Burt is a champion auctioneer, and has raised over $300,000 for charities and causes across Oklahoma and Texas, including the Muscular Dystrophy Association. He is a past-president of the Oklahoma State Auctioneers Association.

He is a dedicated lifelong learner, having earned a doctorate, with honors, from Oklahoma State University and three professional certifications. Much of his time today is spent helping train the next generation of business professionals as an associate professor of Management and Marketing at Oklahoma Christian University. He teaches marketing, organizational design, strategic planning, entrepreneurship, and sales management, at the undergraduate and graduate levels.

In 2007, he was named to the board of directors of the Oklahoma Chapter of the National Speaker's Association.

His wife, Terri, takes an active role in managing the business and an even more active role in managing Dr. Burt and their son, Dalton! They live in Edmond, Oklahoma.

Book Dr. Burt today for a customized, high-energy, high-content program!
See www.burtmarketing.com for more!

Money Back Guarantee!

Thank you for taking this journey with me!

I would never be so arrogant as to present this work as the best book ever written on networking, but I will be so bold as to promise that if you study the principles and techniques discussed in the book and actively apply what is in here, the success of your networking efforts will multiply.

If, however, you do not feel this investment was a good one, and that you didn't get at least ONE idea you could use, I will gladly refund the purchase price. All I ask is that when you mail it back to me at the address shown on www.burtmarketing.com you briefly tell me about how you tried to apply what I suggested in the book and where you feel the techniques failed you. A little market research isn't too much to ask, is it?

On the other hand, I ask that as your networking improves, you share 3% of all your increased profits with me for the rest of your life. Just kidding.

978-0-595-45772-4
0-595-45772-X

Printed in the United States
95025LV00002B/1-75/A

9 780595 457724